PASS THE WORD

50 Years of
Wycliffe Bible Translators

PASS THE WORD

50 Years of
Wycliffe Bible Translators

Ifugao believers study the
translated Scriptures after
the day's work ends.

Editor in chief, Layout and Design:
    Hyatt Moore

Director and Editor:
    Hugh Steven

Assistant Editors and Writers:

Larry Clark	Doris MacDonald
Dave Larson	Carol Schatz
Karen Lewis	Hugh Steven
John Lindskoog	Norma Steven
Alan MacDonald	

Contributing Writers:

Earl Adams	Rose Moore
Clarence Church	Len Newell
David Cummings	Fran Olson
Molly Ekstrom	Dick Pittman
Ben Elson	Cal Rensch
Dick Fry	Myrtle Spencer
Susan Garland	Lynn Todd
Ken Gregerson	Terry Todd
June Hathersmith	Ginny Ubels
Ken Hansen	Ethel Wallis
Margaret Hartzler	Dan Weaver
John Lees	

Typists and Editorial Assistants:

Carol Chase	Heather Eastwood
Nancy Cloud	Valarie Sluss

Art Assistants:

Alice Erath	Julie Klaver
Jeff Girard	Philip White
Ken Harris	

Printing Coordinator:
    Brian Reese

Photo Archivist:
    Nancy Clark

Photographers:
    (See page 144)

Copyright 1984

WYCLIFFE BIBLE TRANSLATORS, INC. HUNTINGTON BEACH, CALIFORNIA 92647

Foreword

How does one tell the story of Wycliffe Bible Translators in one book? Over 900 translations are either in progress or finished. Each one of these is a different story. Each represents a separate culture, complete with its own history, customs and language. Just to study the cultures themselves is fascinating. Then the accounts of people who have been touched by the Word of God in their language are profoundly inspiring. Besides these, there are the moving experiences of Wycliffe workers who've dedicated their lives and skills, working without guaranteed salary or the normal symbols of earthly security, to put the Scriptures into languages that have never been written down.

There's too much to tell in one book. Not only is the quantity vast, but so is the variety. Every situation is unique. The way Bible translation is done in Mexico is not exactly the way it's done in Africa, or Indonesia. The settings are different. The people are different. Their histories are different. There's no one situation that's "typical."

In designing this book our attempt has been to make the picture at least representative. The book is divided into six sections in the same way Wycliffe divides the world: North America, Latin America, Europe, Africa, Asia and the Pacific. From each of these areas we've selected two groups to focus on. In some of these groups the work is almost finished; in others it is still in the initial stages. In some cases, the responsibility for the translation hangs heavily on the Wycliffe member; in other cases, mother-tongue speakers of the language are carrying the bulk of the responsibility. The work might be in the dripping heat of an equatorial jungle, or in sub-zero temperatures of the far north. From the 12 locations shown here, we see a representation of the total work as it stands today — and a picture of the challenge of 3,000 language groups still untouched.

Translating the Bible into another language requires much more than sitting down at a crude table with a native speaker and a copy of an English Bible. It takes linguistic study and modern tools and a team, both on the field and at home.

In the same way, putting this book together was a team effort. Both field and home staff contributed. Many of the photographs came out of missionary slide sets; others were taken specifically for this project. Branch directors assigned field personnel, already busy with their regular programs, to research, write, and gather photographs for particular sections. The editorial staff in the U.S. home office divided up the work, each taking one or two sections, and assuming the responsibility for writing, editing and pulling in all the details from the distant locations. The result you hold in your hand.

Coordination — and teamwork. That's what a project like this requires. That's also what it takes for the whole program of reaching out to those beyond language barriers. That is what Wycliffe is all about.

— *Hyatt Moore*

Helmet mask worn during women's initiation rites — Sierra Leone.

A Budik of Senegal, Africa

Contents

A Paradox of Simplicity

Cameron Townsend seemed to live in a continual paradox. He attempted the impossible, all the while believing in simple solutions. Why? Because he knew God had the answers for impossible situations.

The Lord gave Townsend and Leonard L. Legters the vision to translate God's Word for minority language groups in Mexico. It seemed impossible, but they believed God was in control and would show them the way.

Sitting before closed doors at the Mexican border in 1933, Townsend prayed and Legters hummed the chorus of a song over and over:

Faith, mighty faith the promise sees,
And looks to God alone.
Laughs at impossibilities
And shouts, "It shall be done!"

Suddenly Townsend remembered he was carrying a letter written by Dr. Moises Saenz, a prominent Mexican educator, inviting him to Mexico to "do for our Indians what you have done in Guatemala." After reading the letter from the "father" of Mexico's high school system, the border guard called Mexico City. Permission was granted for the two men to enter the country.

That night, when Townsend and Legters opened their devotional book, they found the words of Exodus 23:20: "Behold, I send an Angel before thee, to keep thee in the way, and to bring thee into the place which I have prepared."

As we look back to 1934, life appears to have been fairly simple. Although money was scarce in those Depression days, dollars seemed to stretch a long way for Cameron Townsend. Once when he was scheduled to leave for Mexico, he had only ten dollars. Ken Pike has put the moment into poetry:

Trailer and wife —
Niece and men —
Coming along.
Work ahead —
Testaments,
Translations,
Five hundred
Languages unwritten
Waiting for us
The world around.
"Leaving tomorrow?"
Lord willing!
"Meaning — if there's money?"
I've got some —
Ten dollars . . . And God.

Ten dollars and God! The Lord blessed Cameron Townsend's faith. The fledgling mission grew quickly and stretched the abilities of the agency that had been handling its funds. Then in 1942 the "Townsend group," as it was sometimes called, prayed that the Lord would double the number of field workers the next year — and He did! The time had come, said the people at the agency, for the "Townsend group" to have its own home office.

William Nyman of Glendale, California, was God's choice to lead the infant home organization, now called Wycliffe Bible Translators (WBT). The retired lumberman donated an apartment over his garage and took no salary for his work. The only paid employee was a secretary, and in the beginning the entire cost of running the office was $150 a month.

The field organization was already known as the Summer Institute of Linguistics (SIL), the name given the training school established by Cameron Townsend in Arkansas in 1934. From those early days, the fundamental distinction between WBT and SIL has been functional. While there is a basic unity in the membership, goals, activities and motivation, the two organizations have different functions. Wycliffe Bible Translators shares the vision for Bible translation with Christians and develops resources needed to see the task completed. The Summer Institute of Linguistics provides academic training and carries out the language work.

WBT recruits, orients and guides interested persons into membership. It is this organization that relates to the Christian community to promote the field work and supply resources to SIL and other field organizations. It also promotes prayer support, but it does not engage in field work as an organization.

SIL maintains SIL schools to provide academic training in linguistic research, literacy work, anthropology and Bible translation. It carries out language field work, including language learning, linguistic analysis and production, literacy, Bible translation and distribution, community work and anthropology. It is this organization that relates to university and academic organizations and to governments.

This book has been especially prepared to celebrate Wycliffe's 50th year. It is our hope and prayer that you will be encouraged to praise God with us. We want to reaffirm that God is faithful and that His promises are true. His Word, translated into all languages on earth, will not return to Him void but will accomplish His eternal purposes.

"Every mother feels she would give all of herself, even die for her children. In many ways, Bible translation is like that. You have a group of people you feel are worthy of your whole life. You give your body, strength, emotion — everything you've got — for their sake and for the Gospel. When you give it all on Christ's behalf, it's easy."
—Joanne Shelter, Philippines.

The Need and Our Role

Train travel in India is an experience few are likely to forget. I was traveling from Bombay to Poona in a vintage steam engine. It was hot! The cool rains and the monsoons had not yet arrived.

In my compartment was a contingent of soldiers. It seemed that we stopped more often between stations than at stations. On one of these occasions they got out their lunch and began eating. Seeing that I had nothing to eat they shared their lunch with me.

As we began eating, I noticed a number of boys outside, begging for any scrap of bread. They were obviously desperately hungry.

One of the soldiers ate his sandwich and then threw the crust out of the window. In a flash one of the boys caught it in the air, but before he could lower his hand another boy had snatched it away from him. I watched with a mixture of pity and incredulity as the boys pounced on that crust, like seagulls fighting for a scrap of food.

I learned an indelible lesson on that trip, and it is this: Just as these youngsters were desperately hungry for physical food, approximately 3,000 language groups await their first taste of the Bread of Life. And that is what Wycliffe Bible Translators is all about.

It is interesting to trace the pattern of the Church's vision for missions through the years. William Carey, that great linguist and Bible translator, took the Great Commission seriously and sailed for India in 1793. He was way out front — the father of the modern missionary movement. Soon the Church caught up with his vision and the missionary effort along the coastal areas of the world began in earnest.

Hudson Taylor came along in the middle of the 1800's. His vision was for the Gospel to be spread to the *interior* of China — not just the coastal areas. But again, he was ahead of his time, and it took the Church a while to adjust to the idea, to catch the vision. But when the Church did catch this new vision, missions to the interior of the world's great land masses began in earnest.

In more recent years, Cameron Townsend caught the vision of getting the Word of God to the minority language groups of the world. He too was ahead of his time and misunderstood. Today there is a ground swell and the Church is beginning to catch a vision for this new frontier. And some tremendous things are happening.

We in Wycliffe see ourselves as a tool for the Church to use in two ways to help accomplish the Great Commission.

Firstly, we are actually *doing* the job of translation through SIL and other organizations. After 50 years of experience we know what the job takes — what it costs, and the training that is necessary. Throughout the years, the Church of our Lord Jesus Christ has stood behind us with its resources and recruits, and with its prayers for the work. The Church is our partner in this specialized task that is an integral part of the Great Commission.

Secondly, we *train* others to do Bible translation. Various segments of the Church have used the SIL schools to prepare their own members for a translation ministry. We gladly share our experience and training facilities with them, for we have a common goal. During the past 50 years, more than 20,000 students have been trained at SIL. A good number have joined our organization, but many others serve with other organizations. And that makes us happy — to see our training being used by the Church at large.

So, any way you look at it, Wycliffe exists to serve the Church — to help the Church with its responsibility to evangelize the world.

Certainly the 200 New Testaments completed by our translators is a significant accomplishment. And yes, work in progress in 700 language groups is a major undertaking. But believe me, all of it is for one and only one purpose: to glorify God by providing the means by which people of all languages can come to Christ and grow in faith as they partake of the Bread of Life in their own language.

— David Cummings, President
Wycliffe Bible Translators

Language: Man's Most Dazzling Possession

The Summer Institute of Linguistics is best understood by tracing its roots to the early, practical sessions on language study initiated by Cameron Townsend at Camp Wycliffe.

Back then the entire science of descriptive linguistics was in its infancy. In 1926 and 1933, the great American linguists Edward Sapir and Leonard Bloomfield had just written their foundational works on language. Those efforts to unravel the mysteries of human speech owed much to the work of European linguists of the nineteenth century who devoted themselves to reconstructing the historical development of the major languages of Europe.

Townsend, however, was especially preoccupied with understanding the languages and cultures of the almost unknown ethnic groups of Latin America. The infant discipline of descriptive linguistics offered hope, and the Summer Institute of Linguistics was born.

From the beginning, the rich panorama of SIL experience has yielded a flood of contributions to the science of language. The bibliography of scholarly publications by SIL members lists thousands of entries. Included are grammars, dictionaries, and papers on syntax, sound systems, semantics, translation (biblical and other), literacy, ethnology and more.

It gives great satisfaction to us as a linguistic organization to reflect on our members' contributions to the early development of the science. The contributions began with Kenneth L. Pike, who pioneered in the areas of phonetics, intonation, tone, syntax and human behavior. Later, other SIL members built upon Pike's foundation and enlarged the understanding of discourse analysis. Currently, new workers are able to build on the work of these scholars as well as study under other leading linguists around the world, thus giving them fresh insights into how people communicate.

The Summer Institute of Linguistics has set for itself the broad task of cooperating with men and women around the world in making language a servant to people rather than a tyrant. This goal involves a variety of specific programs and projects.

A major form of language tyranny around the world is illiteracy. When UNESCO focused world attention on the "Year of the Disabled," it declared illiteracy one of humanity's fundamental disabilities. SIL is in total agreement. Its earliest theoretical studies of language were done with a view toward practical applications for previously unwritten languages.

In 1979 SIL received, on behalf of the government of Papua New Guinea, the UNESCO International Award for literacy. In fact, in most of the nations in which the Summer Institute of Linguistics serves, it collaborates with national authorities on programs of reading and writing.

An example of SIL efforts in bilingual education in Latin America is discussed by Dr. Mildred Larson in *Bilingual Education: An Experience in Peruvian Amazonia*. Literacy methods developed by Dr. Sarah Gudschinsky are reported in *Manual of Literacy for Preliterate Peoples*. Again, this entire effort is directed toward making language "user friendly" and laying the foundations of general education through village level literateness.

The Summer Institute of Linguistics is not only committed to solving the technical linguistic problems; SIL encourages national authors and translators to create a library of literature for people to enjoy. A wealth of traditional oral folklore should be written down before it is forgotten by new generations. On some occasions, SIL cooperates with governmental departments of education to conduct writers' workshops to encourage new authors. Sometimes a village newssheet or a calendar with cultural proverbs can ignite an explosion of popular interest in grass roots education.

In many areas, information flows back and forth across cultural borders by means of translated materials. Field linguists further the process by putting public health, agricultural and other educational materials into the local language. In other areas, members also assist local people in the translation of biblical literature.

Each year two to three hundred new people join the work of the Summer Institute of Linguistics. They come to serve the peoples of the country to which they are assigned. They learn to "bloom where they are planted," to be useful in practical ways in the villages where they live. They may help repair the town well or help develop a cattle-raising program. SIL's aim is to become partners with others in the community and make their language skills available.

In short, the Summer Institute of Linguistics is committed to the highest view of man as reflected in his most dazzling possession — his language. It is the Institute's deep desire to help him harness languages for good.

— Ken Gregerson, President
Summer Institute of Linguistics

Wycliffe Bible Translators And Summer Institute of Linguistics History in Brief

1917: Twenty-one-year-old William Cameron Townsend left college for one year to sell Spanish Bibles in Guatemala. At first sight of him, missionaries declared: "That skinny Townsend won't last two months!"

1919: Realizing the Indians could not read Spanish Bibles, Townsend determined to learn the Cakchiquel language and translate the New Testament. Without knowing it, he had set out to analyze a difficult language — and with no linguistic training. A single Cakchiquel verb can conjugate into 100,000 forms. Eventually, a visiting archaeologist introduced him to the concept of descriptive linguistics.

In March, Townsend opened what was probably the first local Indian mission school in Guatemala. In July, he married fellow missionary Elvira Malmstrom and they settled down among the Cakchiquels. From the beginning, the Townsends developed and encouraged Indian participation and leadership in the work.

1920: Leonard Livingston (L.L.) Legters was the invited speaker at a Cakchiquel Bible Conference. Returning to the United States, he became a champion of Townsend's work and an enthusiastic recruiter and fund-raiser.

1929: At a special completion ceremony of the Cakchiquel New Testament manuscript, Townsend had his parents write in the last two words of the book of Revelation. While the New Testament was at the American Bible Society for publication, Townsend began to generate interest in Bibleless tribes and mission aviation. He was convinced aviation would greatly increase the safety and efficiency of misson efforts.

1931: Townsend, Cakchiquel co-translator Trinidad Bac and a representative of the Bible Society presented a leather-bound copy of the Cakchiquel New Testament to Guatemalan President General Jorge Ubico. Thanking the men, Ubico suggested to Townsend that he translate the New Testament into another Indian language. The presentation was followed by a dedication and distribution of the New Testament in Cakchiquel territory.

Cam and Elvira lived in a Cakchiquel cornstalk house in Guatemala.

Also that year, the psychophonemic method of teaching reading, developed by Townsend, was first used in reading campaigns among the Cakchiquel.

Townsend met Moises Saenz, outstanding Mexican educator in Guatemala. Saenz invited him to come to Mexico to work, later sending a letter of invitation which God used two years later.

1933: In Keswick, New Jersey, and Keswick, England, the Lord gave a special burden for prayer for the unreached peoples of Mexico and the world.

Townsend and Legters went to Mexico to seek permisson to bring in Bible translators. They were allowed to enter the country only after Townsend showed border officials the letter from Saenz.

November 11, the day they entered Mexico, became Wycliffe's annual Day of Prayer.

1934: Remembering his own difficulties in learning the Cakchiquel language, Townsend started a training school for prospective Bible translators at an abandoned farm at Sulphur Springs, Arkansas. It was known as Camp Wycliffe after John Wycliffe, the translator of the first English Bible. Two students came.

Nail kegs provided seating at early SIL sessions.

1935: The second Camp Wycliffe, or Summer Institute of Linguistics, was attended by five students, including Ken Pike.

The first group of translators went to Mexico. Insisting on the highest academic standards, Townsend said: "We will make the scientists sit up and take notice."

The Townsends settled among the Aztecs in a village called Tetelcingo.

1936: Several young women attended the third linguistics course. Two of them, Eunice Pike and Florence Hansen, became the first single women sent as translators.

The Summer Institute of Linguistics was founded by Townsend and his recruits, the first organization ever formed to translate the Bible for minority language groups. The corporation constitution set the significant policy that the Board of Directors would be subservient to the membership.

Five teams began language work in Mexico.

President Lazaro Cardenas visited Townsend in Tetelcingo. He urged Townsend to bring all the young people to Mexico that he could, especially those who would help the Indians in practical ways.

Ken Pike began writing his book on phonetics.

1937: Townsend lectured at the University of Mexico.

Pike began work on his PhD in Linguistics at the University of Michigan, studying under Edward Sapir and Charles C. Fries.

1938: Townsend wrote a book entitled, *The Truth About Mexican Oil*, which was deeply appreciated by President Cardenas and other Mexicans. Townsend mailed a copy of the book to each U.S. Senator and Representative.

1939: SIL hosted an international picnic at Tijuana, Mexico, across the border from San Diego, California. Mexico's President Lazaro Cardenas and various staff members attended.

1940: There were 37 translators working with 18 language groups in Mexico.

Leonard L. Legters died.

1942: Townsend's group was growing, and after he set a goal of 50 new translators, the mission agency that had handled the group's affairs suggested they needed their own sending agency.

To meet this need, Townsend officially established a sister organization to the Summer Institute of Linguistics — Wycliffe Bible Translators. WBT would receive funds and publicize the field work, while SIL would handle training and relationships with foreign governments and universities. William Nyman set up an office for Wycliffe in Southern California.

By the end of the year, Townsend had his 50 new recruits, plus one for good measure.

SIL was invited to the campus of the University of Oklahoma.

1943: Elaine Mielke arrived in Mexico to teach translators' children. She was the first "support worker" in SIL.

1944: Elvira Townsend died.

A new SIL course was begun in Canada.

Language work was begun in North America.

1945: Jungle Camp, designed to teach new recruits to cope with pioneer living, was established in southern Mexico.

1946: Townsend married Elaine Mielke. They moved, along with 19 others, to Peru to head up the new work there.

The first SIL airplane was christened at a ceremony in Lima, Peru. MAF pilot Betty

Mexico President and Mrs. Cardenas were attendants at the 1946 Townsend wedding.

Greene was loaned to SIL and made history as the first woman to fly over the Peruvian Andes.

1947: A plane crash nearly took the lives of the Townsends and their infant daughter when they visited Jungle Camp in Mexico. Townsend's commitment to safe aviation for jungle pioneering was intensified.

1948: Jungle Aviation and Radio Service (JAARS) was established to give aviation and radio support to translators living in remote places. Trips that took weeks by foot and canoe could be made in minutes or hours by plane.

1949: The first Wycliffe film — *O, For A Thousand Tongues* — was produced. Townsend said he wanted "a real top-notch, professional-type movie that would demonstrate to audiences across America just what we are doing and why. It will be the next best thing to visiting the field."

1950: SIL training courses began in Melbourne, Australia.

1951: First New Testament was completed — San Miguel Mixtec of Mexico. The translators were Ken Pike, Don and Ruth Stark and Angel Merecias.

1952: Townsend published his biography of Mexican president Lazaro Cardenas.

The bilingual education system of the Peruvian Ministry of Education was conceived at a luncheon for the Minister of Education, Peruvian educators and SIL members.

1953: SIL work began in the Philippines — the first branch in Asia.

SIL training courses began in England.

1954: The Navajo New Testament was completed — the first North American Indian New Testament translated by Wycliffe.

1955: The first Helio-Courier was given to Ecuador for JAARS to use there. Designed for short take-off and landing, it was ideally suited for jungles and mountains.

Membership in Wycliffe went over 500.

1956: Work began in Papua New Guinea — the first branch in the Pacific.

1959: Membership in Wycliffe went over 1,000. The first second-generation member joined.

1961: The Peruvian Congress voted official commendation of Townsend and the SIL work.

JAARS Catalina Amphibian transports Peruvian Indians to teacher training course.

A Christian businessman gave 256 acres of land in Waxhaw, North Carolina, for JAARS's international headquarters.

William Nyman died.

1962: Work began in Ghana — first branch in Africa.

SIL courses began in Germany.

1963: Modeling the pioneer spirit of Wycliffe once again, the Townsends moved to Colombia to be part of the new work there.

Gaspar Makil and Elwood Jacobsen, Bible translators, were killed in Viet Nam.

1966: September 30, designated "Bible Translation Day," was celebrated in Washington, D.C.

1967: Membership went over 2,000.

1968: The first JAARS helicopter flight took place in Papua New Guinea. A translator who thought he would never need the service because his village was "within driving distance" was the first passenger. A critical case of hepatitis quickly proved to him that helicopter service was not just a "con-venience."

The Townsends accepted an invitation to visit the USSR. It was the first of 11 trips to Russia between 1968 and 1979. As a result, leaders in the Soviet Academy of Science assigned their own linguists to translate I John into several languages.

Hank Blood, Bible translator, died as a prisoner of the Viet Cong.

1969: Wycliffe Associates was incorporated as a lay organization to promote the work of Bible translation.

1970: The Children's Education Department (CHED) began. Wycliffe, of course, had been providing education for its missionaries' children since 1943.

1971: Townsend resigned as General Director of Wycliffe Bible Translators.

1972: With increasing demands for linguistic training, the International Linguistic Center opened its doors in Dallas. In addition to linguistics, advanced programs in translation, literacy and anthropology were offered.

1973: Membership went over 3,000.

1975: The first Japanese SIL was held.

Townsend accepts UNESCO's award at banquet hosted by Cameroon Ambassador Benoit Bindzi.

1979: SIL received UNESCO's Literacy Award for outstanding work done in Papua New Guinea.

The 100th New Testament was dedicated — Amuesha of Peru. The translators were Martha Duff and Mary Ruth Wise.

Membership went over 4,000.

1981: Chet Bitterman was martyred by terrorists in Colombia.

1982: April 23, William Cameron Townsend joined thousands of tribesmen at the throne of God. Billy Graham said, "It is a great loss to the entire Christian world. No man in this century has given a greater vision for being used of God to advance the cause of Christian missions than Cameron Townsend."

Wycliffe linguist Kenneth Pike was nominated for the Nobel Peace Prize.

The Bolivian facilities at Lake Tumi Chucua were turned over to the government. This was the first SIL program to be close enough to completion to begin turning over facilities.

1983: The 200th New Testament translated by Wycliffe personnel was dedicated — Hanga of Ghana, West Africa. The translators were Geoffrey and Rosemary Hunt.

Membership went over 5,000.

I n May, 1931," Cameron Townsend once recalled, "we presented the first copy of the Cakchiquel New Testament to the then President of Guatemala, General Jorge Ubico. Photographers took pictures. Newspapers published articles. It was a delightful occasion. We were happy, but we dismissed the New Testament that remained in the president's possession as a fruitless mantlepiece.

"It was not to be so, however. President Ubico had a desire to help people personally. He would give the poorest peasant a hearing in his office. One day a poor Indian was ushered into the powerful president's office. He had been commissioned by the town elders to ask the 'Great Chief' to prohibit the Protestants from entering their town.

"The president listened to the request made in broken Spanish. Then he stepped over to the bookshelves and took down a nicely bound book. It was the Cakchiquel New Testament. 'This,' he said, 'is in your language. Read it.' The Indian had somehow learned to read Spanish, but he had never seen a book in his own language.

"After reading enough to get what it was all about, he said to the president, 'This is wonderful! Where can I get a copy?'

"'From the very people whom you want to drive out of your town,' retorted General Ubico with a smile.

"The man went home, secured a Cakchiquel New Testament and was born again. The Indian, now a new creation in Christ, would tell people: 'I was evangelized by the president himself!'"

The Complex Structure — It Makes Sense

While the organizational structures of Wycliffe Bible Translators and the Summer Institute of Linguistics may seem confusing to some, the two corporations make sense within their historical context. The decision to function as SIL within host countries had its roots in Mexico — the first country to receive Townsend's fledgling Bible translation organization.

Keenly aware of Mexico's history, Mr. Townsend knew the Mexican government had to assert itself against the power and influence of the established church. As a result, laws had been enacted that prevented churches and other religious groups from owning property, businesses or enterprises of any kind. If a church or other religious organization wished to sponsor a hospital, publish a magazine, operate an orphanage or engage in any other charitable activity, members of that group had to form a separate non-profit corporation.

Thus, in 1935 when Cameron Townsend and his colleagues began their field work in Mexico, they entered the country as a "branch of the Summer Institute of Linguistics," rather than as a religious organization. At that point, the Summer Institute of Linguistics — or Camp Wycliffe, as it was popularly called — was a training school for linguistics and pioneer living held each summer in Arkansas. This identity was acceptable to the Mexico government.

In 1942, the agency that had been forwarding funds to SIL members felt it could no longer handle the work. As a result, Wycliffe Bible Translators was formed to forward funds and relate to Christians at home. The creation of this sister organization was acceptable to the people of Mexico.

Today, although the membership of Wycliffe Bible Translators and the Summer Institute of Linguistics is more than 100 times larger than in 1942, the dual organization structure still works effectively. The Summer Institute of Linguistics does the field work, and Wycliffe Bible Translators is the "resource broker." It is a beautiful partnership. It makes sense.

Ken Pike — Linguist at the Head of the Class

Some say you can't mix religion and scholarship. Others say that those who are deeply religious seldom excel in a secular academic field. If this is true at all, Ken Pike is a bold exception. His life is a combination of reverence for God and the Scriptures and excellence in scholarship.

Ken Pike is a man chosen of God. It is not coincidence that, in 1935, he was one of the first students at the fledgling Summer Institute of Linguistics course. Pike came along at the beginning of both descriptive linguistics and the vision to give God's Word to the hidden peoples of the earth. He was there when the time was right to reach out to minority people groups who needed His Message in a language they could understand.

It is significant that the academic community has recognized Pike for his spiritual goals as well as his goals as a scholar. In 1973 when the University of Chicago presented him with an honorary degree of Doctor of Humane Letters, part of the citation from fellow scholars read as follows, "Since 1935 Kenneth L. Pike has taken literally the injunction to go into all the world and teach the good news of Christ. In dedication to his mission, so that he might understand better the tongues of those to whom he went, and might teach others how to learn those tongues, he became a linguist.... Under his leadership ... the Summer Institute of Linguistics has become the best training ground in the world for field linguistics."

Pike's interest in linguistics arose from practical needs. He has become one of the most significant American theoreticians in the field of linguistics. His interests are wide — phonetics, phonemics, tone languages, general theory. His work on English intonation is still a landmark.

His driving purpose is to obey Christ. Pike notes that Christ not only said that His followers should go and teach (Matt. 28:19), but also that they should love Him with their minds (Matt. 22:37). Ken Pike is delighted with the combination. He delights in helping to spread the good news about Christ around the world. He also delights in helping others to spread it and at the same time making a contribution to the academic community.

One member of that community, French scholar Andre Martinet, read a citation when Pike was awarded Docteur Honoris Causa at the Sorbonne in Paris in 1978. He said, "Kenneth Pike comes from a generation in which one did not receive formal training as a linguist.... His passionate interest in languages ... grew out of theological study and interest in evangelism." Dr. Martinet also observed that spreading the Gospel requires

Ken Pike with his children in Mexico, 1947, addressing academic audience 1983.

translating the divine message into previously unwritten languages. That explains why Ken Pike was the first to present the science of phonology as a technique for developing alphabets for unwritten languages.

Over the past four decades Ken Pike has pursued his research on an extremely broad front. He says he owes much of his academic achievement to his association with the SIL team. His decision to serve the team in Bible translation work has kept him from getting involved in scholastic dead ends. He wants all his study and research to be useful to his colleagues. He is aware that sometimes honors came to him because of the good work his SIL colleagues have been doing. Once, as part of his presidential report to an SIL conference, he burst out with, "God alone could have called out such a strong, competent crew!"

The academic community has recognized Pike's lifelong quest for knowledge and its practical applications. In the early 1980's linguists and educators nominated Ken Pike for the Nobel Peace Prize. One congressman said of Pike and SIL when he nominated him for his high honor, "No other individual or group has done more for some of the most downtrodden of the world."

The life of Kenneth L. Pike is the story of how a monolingual, evangelical young person developed into a scholar renowned in linguistics. Through it all he has considered it his primary responsibility to try to carry out the orders of his boss — Jesus Christ.

SIL Schools — Growing and Serving

The Summer Institute of Linguistics traces its roots back to humble beginnings. In 1934 a few students sat on nail kegs in an abandoned farmhouse in Sulphur Springs, Arkansas, and learned about languages. Their teacher, a visionary named William Cameron Townsend, taught them as much as he knew, based on his research of the Cakchiquel Indian language in Guatemala.

The following year a student named Kenneth Pike arrived at the fledgling school. The combination of Townsend's zeal and Pike's genius and love of research started a worldwide movement. Believing no language group too small or too remote, those who have followed in the footsteps of

14

Townsend and Pike have served minority groups in over 30 countries.

From a rustic school in the Ozarks, the SIL movement has grown to its present academic stature. Nine SIL schools now present linguistic courses in six countries. Because Cameron Townsend insisted on unselfish service motivated by love for God, SIL courses have always been open to any scholar who wished to study descriptive linguistics. There has never been any stipulation that they join the Bible translation movement. The result: SIL has trained over 20,000 students in methods of analyzing languages, creating alphabets and describing grammatical systems of indigenous languages.

In the USA, sessions of SIL are conducted on four university campuses. Beginning with a summer course at the University of Oklahoma in 1942, SIL later opened summer schools at the University of North Dakota (1952) and the University of Washington (1958). For several years SIL also offered linguistic courses in Canada and in the eastern part of the United States. The demand grew for year-round courses in linguistics, and in 1972, SIL started another school in Dallas in cooperation with the University of Texas.

But Townsend's vision included the involvement of linguists from lands outside the United States. He invited enthusiastic scholars from all countries to join him in the task of eliminating illiteracy and giving minority peoples the Bible in their own languages. SIL opened schools in Australia (1949), the British Isles (1953), Germany (1962), Japan (1975) and France (1980).

In addition, mini-SILs have been offered in Brazil, Guatemala, Mexico, Colombia, Nepal, Nigeria, the Philippines and other countries. The courses provide scholars of these lands with an intensive introduction to linguistics and a challenge to study in depth the languages of their own indigenous people.

One student attending the SIL in Oyonnax, France, summed up the feeling of the students when he said, "The courses demand a lot of work, and often you are exhausted at the end of the day. If you did not feel this work had a purpose, if you were not convinced you were here to be better prepared to serve the Lord and to serve others, you would probably give up after the first few weeks. But there is a spiritual life here that refreshes the soul and gives you the strength to keep going. Our times of sharing from the Word of God and of praying and singing together each day are like the still waters to which the Good Shepherd leads us. This atmosphere of Christian fellowship is not only expressed during our daily time of worship, but all through the day, no matter what we may be doing together. I find myself continually being supported and inspired by the love of others."

SIL began with men and women who were willing to sit on nail kegs to learn about linguistics. Today, even though the environment is different, SIL schools continue to train students who share Townsend's vision and Pike's desire for knowledge. These students — ordinary people with a vision and a thirst for knowledge — are the ones who make up the driving force of SIL.

Who Needs a Translation — How Do We Know?

Oluta, Texistepec and Sayula are three villages in the coastal lowlands of Veracruz, Mexico. The Popoluca Indian language is spoken in all three villages, and yet in each case it is a different dialect. Though situated just a few miles from each other, the people in one village do not understand the speech of people in the other villages.

Another group of Popoluca speakers lives in the mountains. Nearly 20,000 people speak Sierra Popoluca in some 30 villages spread over a mountain range that extends from Soteapan to Lake Catemaco. A secluded group, the mountain people are mostly monolingual; few adult males can carry on an adequate conversation in Spanish, and they do not understand the coastal Popoluca languages.

A survey of the four language groups raises the question: Which ones need a translation of the Scriptures?

The answer for the Sierra Popoluca group is obvious. Since the majority cannot communicate well in any language other than their own, they need mother-tongue Scriptures. An SIL team has prepared a New Testament translation for this group. But what about the others?

Margarito Santander was a native of Oluta. Born in 1906, Margarito witnessed most of the twentieth century from the vantage point of an Indian in a changing country. He saw his village depart from its language. In the 1920's his fellow villagers chose Spanish as the language of the future. By the time he died in 1981, fewer than 30 old-timers could still speak the Oluta language. Should we translate the Bible into a dying language such as Oluta Popoluca?

In Texistepec the use of Popoluca is also diminishing. Children speak Spanish in the home, and it is difficult to find anyone under 20 who can speak the Indian language. The Texistepec Popolucas view their language with shame and feel inferior when outsiders make fun of their speech. Their language is gradually dying out. Would the people of Texistepec accept a Scripture translation when they are ashamed of the language and lean toward Spanish?

Sayula presents a different picture. A friendly, outgoing people, they are not ashamed of their language. They have developed a system of stable diglossia; that is, they use Popoluca in their personal lives and Spanish in matters with outsiders. The children still learn Popoluca in the home. How about them? Do they need a translation?

The Summer Institute of Linguistics grapples with these questions in every country it serves. In the case of Oluta, SIL chose not to translate Scriptures because the language is nearly extinct. In Texistepec, while some people might use Scriptures in their own tongue, the general attitude of the people against their dying language makes it appear more practical for them to use Bibles in Spanish, the language of prestige.

The answer for Sayula was to send in an SIL team, and today the people have a New Testament in their version of Popoluca. Even though they may not use the Scriptures in their public meetings, they do use them in their private lives, since they have chosen to retain Popoluca as the language of the home. Abstract concepts, like those of Paul's teaching in Romans, for example, are easier to understand in the language of the heart.

To put it in a nutshell, a language group needs a translation:

— When the majority of the people speak only the language in question.
— When the speakers cannot be adequately reached through any other language.
— When the children still learn the language.
— When the people have a healthy attitude toward their mother tongue and enjoy expressing themselves in it rather than using a trade or national language.

Jungle Aviation and Radio — Tying the Vines

Young Cam Townsend always stopped by Glenn Martin's pasture on the way to high school. He was fascinated by the airplane being developed on that back lot in Santa Ana, California, at the turn of the century. Peering at the fantastic machine, Cam said to himself, "Someday I'm going to fly!"

Years later when Townsend's fledgling organization was placing translation teams in remote areas, he began to dream in earnest of missionary aviation, but there were few who shared his vision.

Then a near-fatal commercial plane crash

A short plane flight can cut days or weeks off difficult travel time.

in southern Mexico spurred him on. Lying near the wreckage, bleeding profusely, Townsend called out: "Get a movie camera! Take pictures before they move us! People need to see how badly we need safe aviation for pioneering in the jungle."

The movie was never made, but the near tragedy of that moment led to the beginning of an aviation program followed by the establishment of Jungle Aviation and Radio Service (JAARS) in 1948.

Today JAARS provides aviation, radio and

15

computer services to its members around the world. Aviation and radio help break through geographic barriers, and computers speed the actual translation process.

The services of JAARS are appreciated not only by SIL members, but also by other missions, government and university officials, and speakers of the minority languages with whom SIL works. Ten appreciative Papua New Guineans of the Sepik Iwam area wrote to JAARS. They are helping translator Marilyn Laszlo "turn over the talk of God" (translate) on a "banana leaf" (paper) in their own language. Marilyn translated their letter:

Hugs (greetings) to you all in the village of Waxhaw. We thank you this morning. We thank you for those canoes which fly about which you made and gave to us to help carry our things and to help carry men and women who are sick, bringing them to the big house which wraps up big sores (hospital). We thank you for this.

Another thing we want to talk to you about is this: when Marilyn ... was close to dead, and she almost did not have a name (died), this flying canoe you made

Skilled mechanics tune JAARS planes to "better-than-factory" condition.

and gave carried her quickly and now therefore she is good. We are also happy for this. We were able to go ahead with our work for the Big Father (God).

You cannot play around with this work you do there. You must tie the vines real good on those flying canoes — it would not be good if we got in and it fell apart. So don't be lazy in your work. Stand up real good and work well.

Everyday we close our eyes and pray for you. May the Big Father be with you giving you help in all things.

With the Aid of the Computer — The Dream Within Reach

Sometimes it seems that few of our dreams will ever become realities. But in the arena of Bible translation, the dream of a fast, efficient, error-free method of handling tedious tasks and prodigious amounts of text material has indeed become a reality.

Many translators leaving for their first assignment now pack a computer among their barrels of clothes, household equipment and books.

A computer? Why a computer?

The answer is time. Translation is a continual round of making corrections and improvements on the translated text. Traditionally, the text had to be retyped every time corrections needed to be inserted into the text.

Back in 1972, Marjorie Crouch, working among the Vagla people in West Africa, was nearly two-thirds of the way through the final draft of the New Testament when she discovered some of the sounds were written incorrectly. It took Marjorie and her translation team nine months of hard proofreading to correct the errors. After that came a complete retyping of the Vagla New Testament.

Today, translators who use computers keyboard their text into their computer once. Then they let the computer do the tedious task of searching for incorrect spellings and making other improvements to the text. It is no wonder the translator sighs with relief when he sees the computer complete in minutes or hours what in pre-computer days would have taken him days and months to complete by hand.

Another significant use of computers is dialect adaptation. Simply put, an operator feeds the New Testament in one language into the computer, and it produces a rough draft in another dialect of the language. The method is not without its own variety of complexities, but it can cut years of time and effort off the production of the second translation.

How does a translator produce Scripture

Computers: useful in translation, accounting, typesetting.

portions or booklets? The quickest way is to use the computer. The translator can add titles to his manuscript, tell the computer what type style to use, and produce a document that is ready to print without retyping and additional proofing at the printshop.

Some languages are written with unique alphabets. Close examination of a computer screen reveals that the letters, numbers and symbols are made by patterns of dots. When a different alphabet is needed, the computer is given an alternate set of instructions and creates a new combination of dots.

The introduction of the computer into translation has produced a whole new set of job descriptions in Wycliffe. Programmers, repairmen, teachers, field managers and others make up the computer team as Wycliffe applies space-age technology to speed up the translation of the Word of God.

The computer often helps make an impossible task possible. A translator in Brazilia who planned to visit his language group two weeks later wanted to take a proof-copy of most of the New Testament to each of 12 villages. Without the aid of the computer, this request would have been impossible, but since most of the material was already on tape, copies of New Testament books began to roll off the printer. Romans took only eight minutes! Two weeks later the translator left with his 12 books. When the villagers received the copies, they were so hungry for the Word of God, they sang: "We will eat it. We will eat it all — not just the soft parts, but the bones and gristle."

The dream has been realized: the computer that has altered the world is bringing dramatic changes to the Bible translation effort.

The Team Approach — It Takes More Than One

"The typical Wycliffe missionary," someone theorized, "probably comes from rural America, specifically from the mid-west. He or she probably believes in the Protestant work ethic, individualism and the American melting pot."

Although this description may fit some, it by no means fits the majority. One quarter of the 5000-plus Wycliffe members don't even come from the U.S.; they come from Finland, Japan, Peru, the Philippines and over 20 other countries. Those from the U.S. are from every state in the union. Anyone who talks with more than one member soon discovers that they hold a variety of viewpoints on virtually every subject. There is no "typical Wycliffe missionary."

Nor is there a "typical Wycliffe profession." Yes, many are linguists and Bible translators, but just as many have other occupations. There are teachers to educate missionaries' children, administrators to provide leadership for field workers and accountants to handle financial matters. Mechanics keep planes and equipment running smoothly; artists illustrate and prepare publicity and book materials for the printing press; and computer scientists play an increasingly important part in financial data processing, manuscript preparation and linguistic analysis.

Wycliffe members come in all sizes and flavors. A brief encounter with a few reveals an interesting variety of people and backgrounds. For example, Neil Anderson was a lumberjack and builder by trade. Now he is a translator working with the Polopa people of Papua New Guinea. Dr. Vida Chenoweth is a leading classical marimbist who has performed at Carnegie Hall. She helped translate the Usarufa New Testament and now heads the Ethnomusicology Department at Wheaton College in Illinois in a joint program with SIL. Paul Duffey was a JAARS pilot. After he suffered a serious injury in a small-plane crash, he and several others developed a new aircraft seat which absorbs much of the impact of a crash. Neil, Vida, Paul and many others exemplify the pioneering spirit

The translated word and the printed page—a pair since the Reformation.

and search for excellence which each member brings to his or her particular piece of the overall task.

With such diverse abilities and backgrounds there is a great potential for lively discussion and even disagreement. Different cultural, denominational and social experiences produce people with very different ideas and ways of doing things. But this is a strength, not a liability. From the very beginning, it has been clear that diversity fosters depth—an added richness, a greater wisdom. Each person brings unique talents to the task and each is an important part of the team.

The Bible translation task is complex and requires the combined efforts of many people working together. The fact that so many kinds of people *can* work together in harmony testifies to the power and creativity of God. He knew the task—and created just the right people to carry it out.

Education for Wycliffe Children — From Packing Box Cupboards to Computers

Packing boxes decorated and stacked to make cupboards. Homemade tables and chairs. A teacher and a handful of students meeting in the wide hallway of a government-owned hotel. This was no ordinary classroom—but then, these were no ordinary students.

The year was 1946, and the children had recently come with their parents to Peru. Their parents, members of the Summer Institute of Linguistics, were translating the Bible for the country's minority language groups. Their life-style was different, but their hopes and dreams for their children were the same as any parents.

Their concern was quality education. As the number of SIL members grew, so did the educational needs of their children, and they looked for ways to meet those needs. Some parents taught their own children using correspondence courses. Others sent their children to boarding schools. As SIL work expanded into other countries, schools were built on many SIL centers, and qualified teachers were recruited to staff them.

In 1970, the Children's Education Department was formed to help families explore all the options. Each family could now make well-informed decisions about the best way to educate their children.

School is individualized for Wycliffe Children.

Providing quality education to fit a variety of circumstances remains a high priority today. However, making decisions that affect a child's education—and perhaps his future—is never easy. Parents are committed to doing everything possible to avoid long separations. But those who choose to teach their children often lose valuable translation time, and their children feel cut off from their peers. Large center schools do not meet the needs of families spread over great distances, and in some cases, they are not feasible because of political considerations. As SIL becomes increasingly international, the needs of students from many different countries must be met.

One creative alternative now being field tested involves the use of microcomputers. Students in scattered locations would be taught by their parents and study with the aid of the computers. They also would meet regularly with itinerant teachers and other students in a central location. This would enable them to stay with their families, receive a good education and yet have valuable peer interaction.

If history is any indication, future challenges will probably be met with the same resourcefulness. SIL regards children as gifts from the Lord and recognizes the great contribution they make to the work of Bible translation. Every effort will be made to keep the work a "family affair."

Wycliffe Associates — The Team Behind the Team

Some 28,000 men and women in the United States and Canada have banded together to provide needed services for Wycliffe and SIL people everywhere. They call themselves Wycliffe Associates.

In the late 1960's, several American businessmen saw the need for lay involvement in Wycliffe's task and organized the team. Since then, a Canadian chapter has been organized as well. From their centers in Orange, California, and Calgary, Alberta, these partners in missions volunteer themselves and their resources all over the world.

You name it, the Associates do it. One of their specialties is funding projects designed to speed the completion of the translation task and show God's love to the people with whom Wycliffe members work. Among their projects have been printing presses, computers, a prosthesis for a Panamanian Indian, linens for furloughing Wycliffe members and cassette players for the blind in the Philippines.

Wycliffe Associates sponsor banquets to fund these projects. The funds also enable them to construct new facilities for Wycliffe around the world. The crew members volunteer their labor, pay their own travel costs and often supply their own tools.

The Associates built a translation center in Irian Jaya, Indonesia. In South America they constructed translation centers in Suriname, Peru and Colombia.

In Australia, one crew built a center for recruiting and training translators in Melbourne; another crew built a translation and language studies center at Darwin to replace a structure destroyed by a 1974 cyclone.

In Huntington Beach, California, a vigorous band of laborers put together 28 two- and three-bedroom apartments to house home-assigned Wycliffe people. Then they turned to a bigger project, a 54-apartment project at the SIL training center in Dallas, Texas.

Other Wycliffe Associates open their homes to traveling Wycliffe people, or they provide lodging for young students whose parents are overseas.

W.A. construction crew in Peru.

And there's more: clean water projects for rural villages, telephones for primitive areas, tap water systems for Wycliffe kitchens. Skilled rank-and-file Christians ready to serve the Lord, provide medical services on the field, fix cars and do plumbing and electrical work.

A willing group of workers, the Wycliffe Associates are at their best when they are helping others—especially those involved in Wycliffe work around the world. No Christian need be without a job as long as the Associates are around to inspire and encourage each one to get involved in the worldwide Bible translation task.

17

Work in the Sending Countries — Home Divisions

Early Wycliffe members were mostly from the United States, with a sprinkling of Canadians. But after World War II, news of Wycliffe's work among the ethnic groups of Mexico spread to England and Australia. Volunteers came from these countries, too, and national councils were formed to represent Wycliffe's work. As the years passed and the councils became more experienced, the Wycliffe Board of Directors gave them wide authority over recruitment, candidate acceptance, fund raising and publicity. News spread still further, and today workers come from nearly thirty different countries.

Countries from which workers come are now known as *sending countries*; every worker from a particular sending country belongs to what has come to be called its *division* — the outgrowth of the early home council. All Canadian members, for instance, belong to the Canada Division; U.S. members belong to the U.S. Division.

Countries where translators work are known as *field countries*; members in field countries are organized into *branches*. Work in Colombia, for instance, is carried out by the Colombia branch. Members of the branch come from many different divisions, or sending countries.

Today's world is much more complex than the world of the 1930's and 40's when Wycliffe was young. The governments of sending countries are increasing their requirements for organizations and individuals. The governments of many field countries are requiring higher academic standards for foreigners working in their countries, and multiplying the rules for granting visas. And the organizational structures of Wycliffe Bible Translators and the Summer Institute of Linguistics are no longer simple.

Each year more people join Wycliffe Bible Translators, requiring increasingly sophisticated systems for processing applications, training members and maintaining lines of communication. It costs more to keep a team in a village than it once did, but at the same time it is possible to provide better-quality Scriptures for a people in much less time. Accumulated experience in Bible translation, tremendous advances in technology and improved training procedures have speeded the process. It appears that dividing the "house" into divisions has also helped make progress toward completing the task.

The Europe area divisions are representative of other divisions around the world. Perhaps more than any other part of the world, Europe's rich history proves that the Word of God in one's language brings spiritual enlightenment and reformation. The legacies of John Wycliffe, Martin Luther and other Bible translators have enriched generations of believers in Europe and around the world. That legacy continues and expands as European Christians, matured by the Word in their own languages, share in the worldwide movement of taking the Word to other countries and other languages.

Workers with Wycliffe Bible Translators have been recruited, trained and sent from Europe since 1952. About 550 workers from 12 countries are now involved in this work. In addition, thousands of partners in these countries give their prayer and financial support.

WBT International has been strengthened by Europe's rich heritage of national and cultural diversity. Many of Europe's citizens are multilingual and, therefore, well suited to linguistic undertakings. Linguistic training courses have been developed in English, German and French. Prospects for greater involvement of Europeans in WBT are encouraging.

There are fourteen Wycliffe divisions in

Europe. These divisions play an essential role in seeing that Scriptures are translated into the vernacular languages of the world.

Each division shares the challenge of Bible translation with Christians in the home country. This involves a myriad of activities — providing speakers for churches, producing literature, organizing prayer groups, representing WBT at mission conferences — all geared toward making known what God is doing through Bible translation and how interested Christians can become involved.

The division takes seriously its responsibility for the well-being of its members as well, working closely with them from their first inquiry into WBT to their retirement.

Home-assigned personnel play an important part in keeping their co-workers on the field (left). They also help develop prayer and financial support and encourage others to join in the Bible translation task.

(Below) A children's evacuation center during World War II, the British Wycliffe Centre in Horsleys Green, England, can accommodate 300 people for SIL courses and is the headquarters for Wycliffe in Britain.

In varying degrees, divisions aid field personnel in the production of materials. Some, like the British Division, help in the actual mechanics of getting a New Testament ready for printing. Here an artist pastes up translated Scripture (top right).

Mechanics, bookkeepers and file clerks — often the unsung members of the team — all play an important part in the overall task of Bible translation. Here Margaret Wood helps keep track of candidate information in the British Division (bottom).

British Division

Located at beautiful Horsleys Green in Buckinghamshire, England, the British Division shares the grounds with the British SIL school. Here, initial inquiries and applications are processed, British members' finances are kept in order, and some New Testaments are prepared for publication.

The SIL courses provide linguistic training not only for Wycliffe members but for students anticipating service with more than 30 other mission groups. Approximately 250 students representing some 20 countries attend the course each year.

Richard Fry, British Division director, explains the year-round role of the Horsleys Green Centre: "The Wycliffe Centre functions like a motorway services area. Some Christians pass through en route to overseas assignments, and we provide the practical linguistic training that equips them for their work. Experienced overseas workers return for refueling and retooling. Other Christians come for diagnostic service to find out if God wants them involved in Bible translation or literacy work."

Though division work is often behind the scenes, it is exciting and challenging. "As we hear from around the world of progress in linguistic work and Bible translation, we realize the privileged part we have in taking new dignity and fullness of life to neglected peoples," says Fry.

Summing up the task of the division, Fry says, "I believe our job in British Wycliffe is to inspire prayer, find new workers and channel financial support. Constantly before us are the 200 million people who still need God's Word in their own language."

German-speaking students from several European countries come to Holzhausen for linguistic and translation training (left and right). In Europe, SIL courses are held in England, Germany and France.

Northern Ireland Regional Program

As interest in Wycliffe has grown in Britain, the division has sought to "regionalize" its outreach in the countries that make up the United Kingdom. The Northern Ireland Regional Program is one example.

On Saturday evenings, the home of Ian and Claire Gray, Wycliffe Regional Representatives, is packed with young people. These young people are eager to know more about the world beyond Northern Ireland and about the possibilities of becoming involved in Christian work overseas. During the course of the evening they might learn a little about the mysteries of language or how to eat Ghanaian food with one's fingers.

On other evenings, international students use the Grays' home for their get-togethers. These students, who attend local colleges, come from countries such as Malaysia, Nigeria, Namibia and Ethiopia. The Grays pray that some will catch a vision for their own people while in Northern Ireland.

Twice a year, 70 or more young people leave the city to experience life on a farm. Here they learn to bake bread, kill chickens and change a car tire. They go on a survival hike and try their skills at horseback riding. They look at a bit of phonetics and grammar and attempt to solve some translation problems. Those who are interested can attend a one-day "Schnuffel" course where they can seriously "sniff" at linguistics.

Work for the Grays is more than exotic dishes and fireside chats. They also write and publish a newsletter, write numerous personal letters, speak at church meetings, answer telephone inquiries and lead prayer groups. Their desire is to see young people go and give the Scriptures to those who still need it in their own language.

Austria Representatives

When Austria Representatives Wolfgang and Erna Binder talk about the Philippines, you can sense how much they enjoyed living there. And when they talk about their current work in Austria, you discover they are equally enthusiastic. "The important thing," says Wolfgang, "is to know why you are where you are." Wolfgang is indeed certain why he and his family are now in Austria, and confidently outlines his ministry.

At the top of his list is evangelism. Since many of the people he meets lack a basic understanding of Wycliffe, Christian missions and, in many cases, the Christian Gospel, Wolfgang's ministry is to lay a basic foundation in these areas. Much of his ministry involves Bible teaching "wherever the Lord opens the door." Add to this his commitment to teach about missions and Austria's part in it, and one can see the Binders have a challenging ministry.

Wolfgang and Erna see themselves as "seed sowers." Says Earl Adams, area director for Europe, "The work of the Binders and other representatives is one way Wycliffe can share internationally. The education of pastors and students toward world mission opportunities is one of our first priorities in Austria and the rest of Europe."

The Binders feel their work in Austria contributes as much to worldwide Bible translation as did their work in Asia. "It was Wycliffe's emphasis on teamwork that first attracted us to this organization," say Wolfgang and Erna. "In this spirit we now serve as support workers where once we served as translators. As long as we see that the job we do is necessary, we'll do it."

Belgium Division

Tucked away in the recesses of the impressive Belgium Bible Institute building in Leuven is the Wycliffe office. Here, Elisabeth "Lies" Kruis spends part of her time as Wycliffe's Belgium Representative.

Originally from the Netherlands, Lies came to the Bible Institute as a student. It was here she learned about Wycliffe's work and decided to go to England to take SIL's linguistics course. After completing the course, she felt translation work was not for her and returned to Belgium, where she accepted a position on staff at the Bible Institute. However, the Lord still had a role for her in Wycliffe — that of serving on the local Wycliffe committee.

Now, in addition to her jobs as a Dutch language instructor and the Bible Institute's registrar, she finds herself deeply involved with Wycliffe. She handles member finances, sends out donor receipts and keeps up with routine correspondence. She also arranges "Mini-SILs" for prospective applicants, distributes WBT literature, handles contacts with churches and arranges film showings and meetings.

Other Wycliffe committee members also spend an evening or two each week praying for the work and helping Lies handle some of the work.

The Belgium Division, begun in 1972, now has three families on field assignments. Evangelical Christians in Belgium make up only one-half of one percent of the population, which makes growth within the division more difficult than in some countries. But this does not deter Lies in her presentation of the challenge of Bible translation. "I accept the fact that we are small," she says, "yet, we *can* see growth, and the Lord *is* blessing."

Many Wycliffe members assigned to French-speaking countries first study French in France or Switzerland. Besides learning the language, they develop cross-cultural living skills. Jim and Jan Tyhurst (below), now assigned to Cameroon, studied in Albertville, France.

Gunnell Gustafsson, manager of the Swedish Wycliffe office and an experienced executive secretary (right), is representative of many who bring skills from other successful careers to their service with Wycliffe.

"Mini-SILs" are one or two-week introductions to linguistics and Bible translation. They are held in several countries for students considering involvement in the Bible translation effort. Danilo Valla, Italian Wycliffe representative, teaches at a Mini-SIL course in Rimini, the first course to be held in Italy (below).

Italy Representative

Danilo Valla, Wycliffe's representative in Italy, exudes originality and boundless energy.

Danilo was converted through the witness of Finnish missionaries who befriended him and shared their faith. At first Danilo resisted their message. But when they returned to Italy the following summer and contacted him again, Danilo was touched by their genuine love and concern, and he accepted Christ into his life.

Danilo went with his new-found friends to Finland to study at a Bible college. Later, he learned of Wycliffe at "Mission '76" in Lausanne, Switzerland. Hoping to become a Bible translator, Danilo completed his university degree in linguistics and Hebrew. He then attended the British SIL course, but, unable to meet the English requirement, he turned his attention to sharing the vision of Bible translation with Italian Christians. In early 1981, he became Wycliffe's official representative in Italy.

Today, Danilo devotes many hours to working with young people, helping them find their place of service in God's world. To assist them in preparing for overseas work, he conducts a training school in his own home — an institute for the study of biblical languages. He also teaches the Bible in many of the Christian assemblies throughout Italy. His regular newsletter for those interested in Bible translation illustrates his creativity. His is the only Wycliffe publication offering lessons in modern Chinese and a systematic study of the books of the Pentateuch!

Danilo is convinced of the potential in Italy's churches. Though only one person, he is multiplying his vision by inspiring others to become involved in the task of Bible translation.

Divisions

AUSTRALIA
AUSTRIA
BELGIUM
BRAZIL
BRITAIN
BRUNEI
CAMEROON
CANADA
DENMARK
ECUADOR
FINLAND
FRANCE
GERMANY
GHANA
GUATEMALA
INDONESIA
ITALY
JAPAN
KOREA
MEXICO
NETHERLANDS
NEW ZEALAND
NORWAY
PERU
PHILIPPINES
PORTUGAL
REPUBLIC OF IRELAND
SINGAPORE
SOUTH AFRICA
SWEDEN
SWITZERLAND
UNITED STATES

LATIN AMERICA

Here's where Wycliffe's Bible translation movement got its start — first in 1917 with young Cameroon Townsend selling Spanish Bibles in Guatemala, and then in the mid-30's with Townsend, now a seasoned translator, entering Mexico with a handful of eager young students.

The pattern developed in those early days and has continued, with modification as needed, until now: SIL works in close cooperation with national and local governments, offering its services in the areas of linguistics, literacy, anthropology and practical help projects. These activities involve continuing contact with educators and officials at all levels of government and, of course, service to the minority language groups, many of whom live in humble conditions.

The Latin America Area includes Central and South America — everything between the southern U.S. border and Tierra del Fuego. It even includes Easter Island, 2000 miles west of South America in the Pacific Ocean. United by its Spanish and Portuguese heritage, Latin America nevertheless demonstrates tremendous variety, both in people and in geography. Mexico is heir to rich cultural traditions going back to the Mayans, the Toltecs and the Aztecs; most of western South America reflects Incan influence; and the great Amazon basin is home to hundreds of other Indian peoples.

Wycliffe teams serving with the Summer Institute of Linguistics have begun work in some 380 languages. These language groups range in size from less than 200 speakers, like the Mura-Piraha in Brazil, to many hundreds of thousands, like the Highland Quechua of Bolivia. As the result of SIL work, over 100 New Testaments have been completed and published in languages of the Latin America area. A number have been done by other agencies, and yet 181 languages still remain to be studied. Some of these remaining language groups may be able to use translations already in existence, but most will need separate translations.

While much work remains in some Latin American countries, the work in other countries, such as Bolivia, is nearing completion. This follows another pattern developed by Townsend: translators complete the task and move on to other groups still needing Scriptures in their own language.

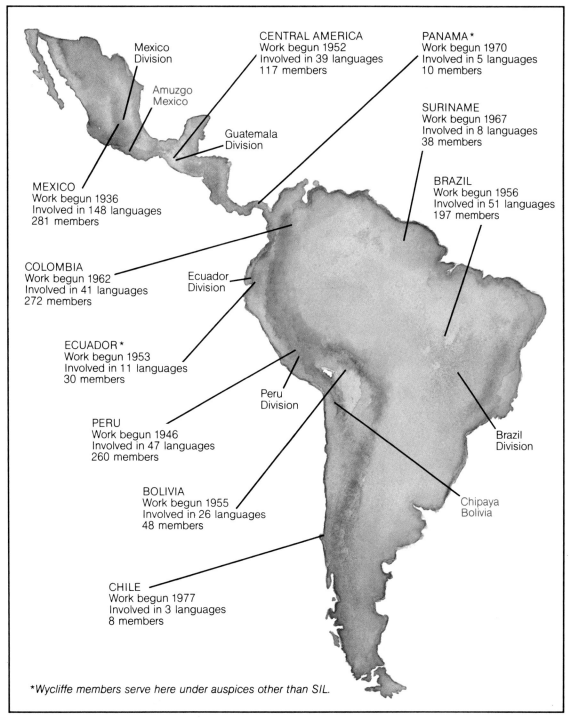

Mexico
Division

CENTRAL AMERICA
Work begun 1952
Involved in 39 languages
117 members

PANAMA *
Work begun 1970
Involved in 5 languages
10 members

Amuzgo
Mexico

SURINAME
Work begun 1967
Involved in 8 languages
38 members

Guatemala
Division

MEXICO
Work begun 1936
Involved in 148 languages
281 members

BRAZIL
Work begun 1956
Involved in 51 languages
197 members

COLOMBIA
Work begun 1962
Involved in 41 languages
272 members

Ecuador
Division

ECUADOR *
Work begun 1953
Involved in 11 languages
30 members

Peru
Division

PERU
Work begun 1946
Involved in 47 languages
260 members

Brazil
Division

BOLIVIA
Work begun 1955
Involved in 26 languages
48 members

Chipaya
Bolivia

CHILE
Work begun 1977
Involved in 3 languages
8 members

*Wycliffe members serve here under auspices other than SIL.

The Amuzgo of Mexico

We were excited about the Scriptures," said the old Amuzgo man, remembering the days when God's Word first became available in his language. "Every trip to the cornfield was an opportunity to witness. I'd say to my fellow Christians, 'Pray for me, Brother. I'm going out to hoe corn for Old Jose.'

"I'd place the Gospel of Mark in my shoulder bag and go to work with a group of Amuzgo men. When the sun touched the middle of the sky, we'd sit down in the shade of a tree and pull out our tortillas. Then I'd take out my book and begin to read.

"'Hey, what's that?' someone would say.

"'Well, it's God's Word in our language,' I'd say. 'Would you like to hear some of it?'"

With the spontaneous witness of men excited about God, the early Amuzgo church sprang into being. The Amuzgos were amazed to learn that God could actually address them in their own language, that He heard them, and that He loved and cared for them. Such excitement about the Gospel impelled the first Amuzgo believers to tell others the good news of the Gospel wherever they happened to meet another Amuzgo — in the cornfield, in the market or on the trails.

But before any of this happened, someone needed to translate the Scriptures into the Amuzgo language.

A gasoline lantern in a dark Indian village drew curious Amuzgo boys to the home of Cloyd and Ruth Stewart. During the late 1940's, before electricity brightened their villages, Amuzgo boys had little to do during the long, pitch-black evenings, and since the translators' house was the only "bright" spot in the village, they strolled by to see what was happening. Some went in and huddled around the table where Cloyd sat with his wife. Others stood out on the porch, concealed in the shadows.

"We never pressured them to come inside," Cloyd said, "but one night a young man named Agapito had enough courage to come in. He had heard we had a book that told about God, and he listened as I explained the Gospel in Amuzgo. The message of God's Word whetted his appetite, and he returned each night to listen to these new and wonderful words. In time he learned to read for himself."

As Agapito returned night after night to Cloyd's home, his mother began to notice her son's unusual pattern. Each afternoon when Agapito came home from the fields, he would bathe, put on clean clothes, eat his evening meal, then without a word, disappear. Finally she asked what he was doing and where he was going.

"I'm going to the translator's house," said Agapito.

A look of horror crossed her face. "My son," she cried in alarm, "you know I've just become a widow. If anything happens to you, who will take care of me?"

Agapito's mother feared the *cachupay*, the Amuzgo term for an outsider. According to Amuzgo belief, it was the *cachupay* who vandalized the cemetery, disinterred recently buried people and ate their flesh. This explained the *cachupay*'s white skin. Besides, Agapito's mother had heard someone say he saw a forked tail wiggling from the bottom of Cloyd's jeans. Someone else had said he had seen two horns under Cloyd's hat. She felt as frightened as the young

children who ran in terror whenever they saw Cloyd and Ruth in the streets.

"Please don't go back to that man's house," Agapito's mother pleaded. "You know all the things people say."

"Yes, mother," said Agapito calmly. "I know what they say, but he's got a Book that tells us about God and Jesus. Not the Jesus hanging on the old termite-eaten cross in the church, but the Jesus who was buried and rose again. He's alive, Mother!"

Realizing she couldn't dissuade him, she said, "Well, please be careful."

"I will," Agapito promised. "If I see anything amiss, I won't go back anymore."

But Agapito never found anything amiss at the Stewart home. "Our home was always open to the people," Ruth Stewart says. "They could see all that went on. It was inconvenient for us, but it won the confidence of the people. We found that

having open house in the evening for the young men furnished us time to be a casual witness for Christ."

Soon young Agapito was a leader in the fledgling church. He became a translation helper and with others took an active part in preaching the Word Sunday by Sunday.

From the beginning, the Amuzgo church was led by Amuzgos. Amuzgo believers witnessed to their non-believing neighbors, and when they came together for worship, it was the Amuzgos who chose the hymns, led in prayer, and taught and preached the Word. At the close of a Sunday service it was common to hear someone say, "Well, brother, can we meet at your home next Sunday?" The reply was almost always, "Yes."

In this way, the Amuzgo church met Sunday by Sunday in one another's homes. Each of the believers counted it a great privilege to take a turn at hosting the church.

The Amuzgo Christians took the Word of God seriously. They regarded it as a message from God to be studied and lived out in their daily lives. When they came to the closing chapters of Mark's Gospel, the believers began to question what Jesus meant about being baptized.

One Sunday afternoon the believers met Cloyd on the trail as he returned from an errand. Their faces were radiant!

"The Lord is wonderful!" Agapito said.

"He is indeed!" said Cloyd.

"You don't understand," said Agapito.

Cloyd looked at the young Christian leader and said, "What are you talking about? What don't I understand?"

"We washed ourselves."

"You washed yourselves? What do you mean?" asked Cloyd.

With a triumphant smile, Agapito said, "Naro, Old Peter, Lame Amado and I went to the river. We went to wash ourselves as Jesus told us to. Old Peter and Lame Amado stood on the shore while Naro and I walked out into the river. I asked Naro, 'Do you believe in God?' 'Yes!' he said. Then I asked him if he believed God loves him, that God sent his son Jesus and that when Jesus died on the cross it was for his sins. He said 'Yes' to each question."

"Sounds good," said Cloyd. "Then what did you do?"

"Because the Bible says to wash people in Jesus' name and in His Father's name, and in the Holy Spirit's name, I washed Naro and then after he had asked me the same questions, Naro washed me. When we came out of the water, I brought back Old Peter and Naro brought back Lame Amado, and we washed them in the name of the Father, the Son, and the Holy Spirit. We are grateful to God and happy to have obeyed Him."

These four Christian men had never seen a

baptismal service. No one influenced them; no one imposed an outside ritual on their culture. They simply read the translated Scriptures and responded to the prompting of the Holy Spirit. Then, because they had obeyed the Lord, they came away rejoicing.

Gradually, as Amuzgo Christian leaders used the translated Scriptures, the infant church grew. Eventually their numbers grew to the point where their tiny homes could no longer hold them. Instead of splitting into several small groups, they decided to meet in one place. They purchased a house and widened it to make room for the congregation.

Looking back on 28 years with the Amuzgo people, Cloyd says, "I'm a poor stick, but God chose to use me. He has blessed the Amuzgos to the honor and glory of Jesus Christ. They came to know Him through the Word translated into their language, not through anything we did.

"The most precious memories we have of working with the Amuzgos are of the times we had to leave the village. To miss the hot sun, we would leave around 2 a.m. during a full moon and trek out by horse and mule to the nearest town, about eight hours away. Even at such an hour, the believers would come to say good-bye. After someone had led in prayer, they'd come up, shake hands and say, 'God go with you, Brother. Maybe I'll not be here when you come back. But if I'm not, I'll meet you in the Father's house.'"

His voice breaking with emotion, Cloyd said, "They never had such a hope until the Word reached them in their own language."

Lame Amado

Amado was born with two good legs. As he grew, he developed into a normal Amuzgo child who loved to play and run. One day young Amado was sent to cut firewood on a neighbor's land. A man who coveted the property picked up a chunk of wood and hurled it at the boy. The wood struck Amado's thigh and damaged the nerve. Amado grew, but one leg remained shorter than the other, and he was given the nickname Lame Amado.

Years later, when Amado was older, he learned that Cloyd and Ruth Stewart had come

to live in his village. At first he avoided the outsiders. Then he learned that the Stewarts had come to translate the Scriptures into the Amuzgo language. Gradually Amado overcame his fear, became friends with the Stewarts and eventually joined others in worshiping the Lord.

As he went to church Sunday by Sunday, Amado heard the Scripture portions the Stewarts had translated and felt sad — he couldn't read. How could he ever enjoy the Bible?

At first Amado sat with the men and memorized the Scriptures as they read them. He did store some of the Word in his heart, but he wanted more. Finally, when the entire Amuzgo

New Testament was printed, Amado brought his copy to Cloyd Stewart.

"Brother," said Amado, "where does it say that all have sinned and come short of the glory of God?"

Cloyd found the place and underlined it. Amado marked the place with colored thread. He asked the location of other key verses and marked each with a different colored thread or a piece of grass.

Gradually Amado developed a mental file box. Each thread or piece of grass signaled a different verse. Now he was ready to teach himself to read. Carefully, Amado looked at the spaces between the words and painstakingly figured out the letters. Little by little he learned

to read.

Today Amado stands before the congregation of believers and reads the Word to them. He is also an evangelist among his own people. He climbs up and down hills carrying the Word to other villages. His love for God bubbles over as he uses every opportunity to tell others about the Lord. Nothing stops him, not even his crippled leg!

Cloyd says when he begins to complain about the muggy weather or a few inconveniences, the Lord reminds him of Lame Amado — the man who taught himself to read; the man who ignores a lame leg and travels for God over rough mountain trails to tell others about Christ.

The Amuzgos Learn to Read

The Amuzgo people of Mexico had never seen their own language in writing before linguists arrived from the Summer Institute of Linguistics. Translators Cloyd and Ruth Stewart developed an alphabet, translated Scripture and taught some of the people to read. Nurse-linguist Amy Bauernschmidt helped analyze the language, worked on translation and helped the people with medical problems. But it was Marjorie (Marj) Buck, a quiet, reserved New Yorker, who encouraged the majority of Amuzgos to read.

Though Marj has her roots deep in missions (one uncle was a missionary in China and another uncle served in Africa), she doesn't fit the stereotype of the outgoing, adventuresome missionary. Instead, she has stayed behind the scenes for 30 years as a gentle but persistent worker in literacy, motivating the Amuzgos to read and create literature in their own language.

When Marj arrived in the Amuzgo village of Xochistlahuaca, she found a shy, friendly people who spoke only Amuzgo. These people lived just 100 miles south of the resort city of Acapulco and 40 miles inland from the Pacific Ocean, yet they kept themselves secluded from the outside world.

As Marj struggled to learn Amuzgo, she thought almost constantly about literacy. From her first days with the people, she used a notebook and showed anyone who would listen the words of their language. She started making primers and typed up reading lessons.

The few Amuzgos who read Spanish were able to transfer their knowledge of letters and sounds to their own language. But because Amuzgo has a more complex alphabet than Spanish, many found it difficult to correlate the sounds of their spoken language with the letters they saw on paper. Some caught on with very little help; others needed a systematic method that would teach one thing at a time and progress at a rate they could handle.

Marj took on the huge challenge of preparing primers and then persuaded and encouraged Amuzgos that no matter what their age or lack of schooling, they could learn to read.

On dark evenings, the Coleman lantern at Marj and Amy's home attracted the village children. Drawn like moths to a light, the children flocked to the house and filled up every bench and chair. The two women welcomed them and showed them *National Geographics* magazines. Marj also used this opportunity to teach reading. "Usually I'm quite reserved," says Marj, "but when it comes to teaching Amuzgos to read, I become aggressive."

Marj discovered that the only Amuzgos who wanted to read were those interested in the Scriptures Cloyd and Ruth Stewart were translating. Most of the others lacked the motivation to strain over the written words of their language.

After living in the village of Xochistlahuaca for several years, Marj and Amy moved to the nearby town of Ometepec. Their hope was that by living outside the Amuzgo area, they could devote their full energies to Scripture translation. Nevertheless, Marj could not resist giving much of her time to Amuzgo young people who were seeking to improve their reading skills.

Many of these youths blossomed into future leaders in the Mexican community. One became a doctor; two are now registered nurses; another is

a teacher in bilingual education. Another graduated from the University of Mexico City and became a veterinarian; recently he wrote a booklet in Amuzgo to help his people care for their cows.

Marj looks at these young people — now successful in their chosen fields — and sees that she and Amy have influenced the Amuzgos' lives because they learned to speak the Amuzgo language. Marj and Amy took time to listen to these young people, to pray with them, and to read and study the Scriptures with them. Their doors were always open when Amuzgos came to visit.

Marj has had her down moments, too. At one point in those early years she realized that even though 200 people could read in Amuzgo, they represented only a fraction of the 20,000 Amuzgo people. Many of the women knew nothing about

reading, and most of the men lacked the time and interest to become good readers.

Mixed emotions flooded Marj whenever the time drew near for her and Amy to go away for a translation workshop. As much as she wanted the Amuzgos to have the Scriptures, she longed to stay in their villages to prepare them to read the Bible.

The answer came when Christian leader Agapito approached her. "Who is going to teach reading while you're gone?" he asked.

"I just shrugged my shoulders," Marj said. "I had dreamed of the day when Amuzgos would be teaching each other, but nobody seemed ready, and I didn't know how to help them teach each other.

"But Agapito's question spurred me on and I

decided to ask four of my best pupils to teach the next reading class. I divided the other pupils among those four teachers, who did an excellent job! Afterward I walked home feeling elated and free because Amuzgos were at last teaching their fellow Amuzgos to read!"

The arrival of the printed New Testament in 1974 spurred other Amuzgos to learn to read. The Bible was in their own language, and many wanted to know what God had to say to them.

Marj challenged her pupils to read all the way through a complete book of Scripture, and some did. Then two teenagers, Joel and Abel, began reading through the entire New Testament. While Marj was in Oklahoma on her summer assignment at SIL, they wrote her letters telling of their progress. Joel reported he had finished reading

An Amuzgo teenager (far left) demonstrates his ability to write in his own language. Reading specialist Marjorie Buck has put most of her life into teaching Amuzgos to read.

Amuzgo men (left) work at typing their language, putting their words on paper. An intelligent people, the Amuzgos are quick to learn new skills and many have excelled in professional work.

Long bench-desk serves new writers (below). SIL linguist Amy Bauernschmidt instructs them in literacy. The dresses with their intricate designs are everyday wear for Amuzgo women and distinguish them from other Indian groups.

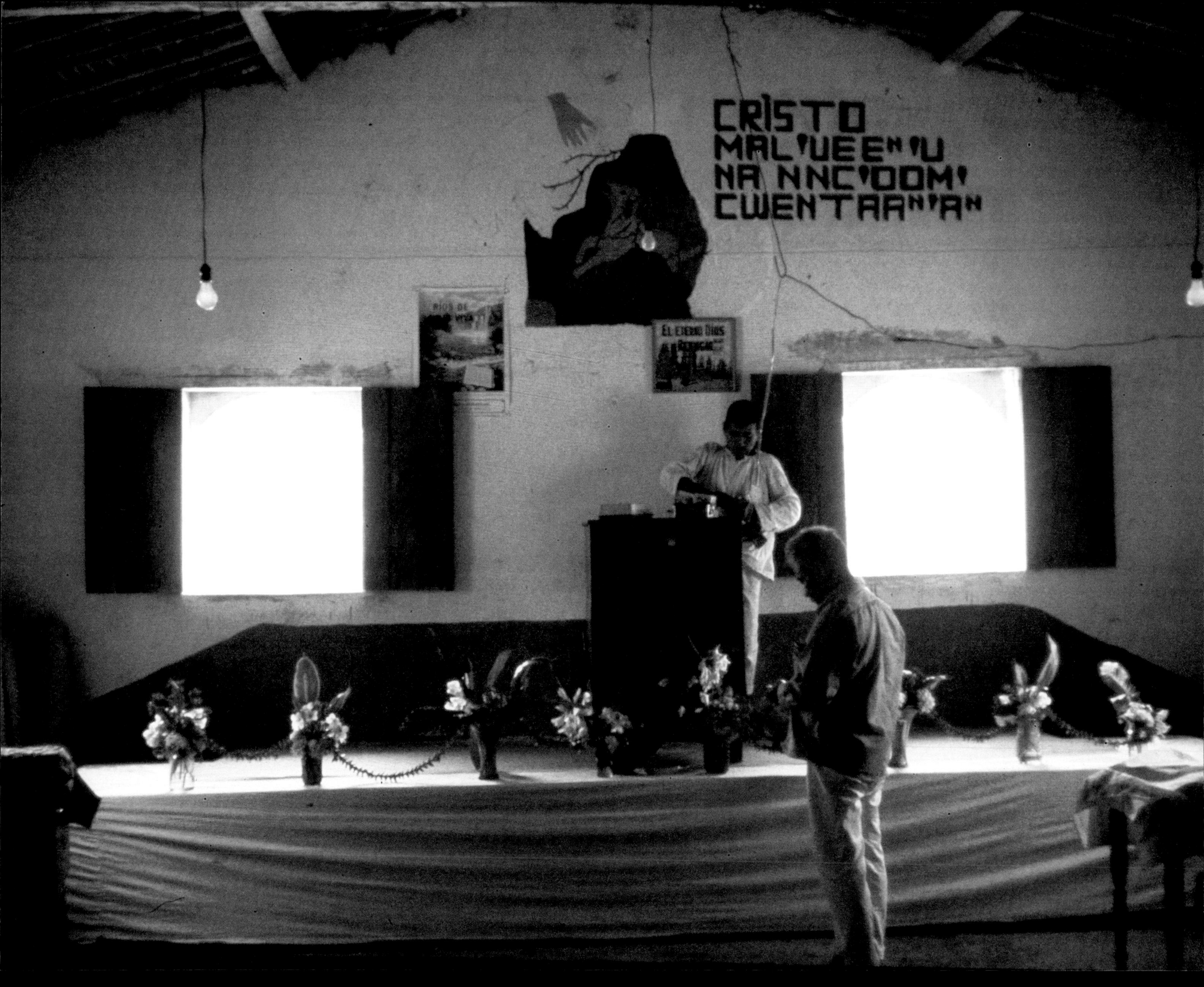
CRISTO
MAL'UEEn'U
NA NNC'OOM'
CWENTAAn'An

the New Testament.

"I could tell he had been reading it," said Marj. "His letters sounded just like a letter from the Apostle Paul. His salutations and endings were the same.

"Another man in his late 20s, who had a family and was kept busy with field work during the day, took two years to read his New Testament through by candlelight. Later he became a lay preacher. The ones who learned to read became the ones who now preach and teach the Word," said Marj.

Marj's patience and persistence in teaching has borne spiritual fruit. She remembers one reading class when an awkward teenager joined the class. The other students were well into their lessons, but Chico didn't know one letter from another. He couldn't even copy letters because he lacked hand-eye coordination.

Although Chico found it difficult to learn to read, he was persistent. Even with Marj's special help he learned slowly. When the classes ended a month later, Chico still had made little progress. But as he walked away, he reached out and shook Marj's hand. "I'm going to come to church," he said.

"Why did he say that?" Marj wondered. "He's never come to church before. Maybe he is just expressing appreciation and wants to say something that will please me."

Not long afterward when Marj walked into church, Chico was there. From then on he attended every service, and a few months later he accepted Christ as his Savior.

"I didn't think I'd helped him much," said Marj. "But one day he said to me, 'No one ever helped me learn to read before.' My kindness to him

during the reading classes became a stepping stone for him to attend church and to accept Christ."

Her many kindnesses have paid off. In the past 30 years the Amuzgos have responded to love in action, and today many are believers because they have seen Christ in the lives of people like Marj Buck.

Marj compares herself to the boy who gave his lunch of five loaves and two fishes to Jesus to feed the crowd. "I didn't have a lot to offer," she explains. "I was only teaching a handful of people at a time to read, but God took that little bit and now He is beginning to multiply it."

As other Amuzgos teach one another to read the New Testament, her work, just like the loaves and fishes, is being multiplied in thousands of lives.

37

Bolivia — Finishing the Course

On April 3, 1982, the Summer Institute of Linguistics took a historic step toward the completion of its work in Bolivia: it turned over its Amazon jungle education facilities at Lake Tumi Chucua to the Bolivian Government. The ceremony was attended by the Bolivian Ministers of Education and Health, ambassadors and other high government officials.

Said Dave Farah, SIL's Director of Government Relations, "In a few years we'll be leaving Bolivia. We've nearly finished the linguistic and other goals that were outlined for us by the Bolivian government in 1954. We leave with deep appreciation to the Bolivian people for their strong support and cooperation over these 27 years."

The event at Tumi Chucua is significant in SIL's 50-year history. It is the first time a branch has completed the majority of its work and turned its facilities over to the government. The branch has published eight New Testaments already and had significant input into a ninth — the Aymara. There are six to go. The group plans to finish the rest of the work by 1985 and leave Bolivia.

A cable from Wycliffe founder Cameron Townsend to Bolivia's President General Celso Torrelio was read at the Tumi Chucua gathering. Sent just days before Townsend died, it read, "I express to you my gratitude for the 27 years of cooperation with the people of Bolivia which has resulted in a very important accomplishment for linguistic science, bilingual education and the translation of portions of the Bible for many Indian languages.... We love Bolivia. As we near the conclusion of our studies in Bolivia, we present to you the center of our activities which we have constructed in Tumi Chucua. We hope it will serve you as a center for Indian education and also as a monument to the benefit of the cooperation between our people for the good of the indigenous groups. We honor your glorious country!"

The Minister of Education and Culture, Lt. Col. Juan Vera Antezana, who accepted the gift on behalf of the Bolivian people, responded, "SIL has made it possible for us to communicate and work together with people in 17 language groups."

During its 27 year history, SIL's center at Tumi Chucua has been used to train bilingual education teachers and paramedics. Today, 53 indigenous teachers trained at the center instruct more than 1,000 children in 43 schools. Many have also learned to write and edit and are equipped with typing skills and simple publishing techniques that can be used in their home environment.

The Tumi Chucua center has also provided classes on how to raise cattle and poultry and how to repair outboard motors. Of particular significance are the 37 ethnic minority people who have been trained as radio technicians.

After turning Tumi Chucua over to the Bolivian government, the remaining SIL personnel moved to Cochabamba, a city in central Bolivia. This will be their center of activities until 1985 when they expect to complete the work and leave.

Many SIL members, particularly those who have worked in Bolivia for most of the 27 years, have found it difficult to leave. Bolivia has been home for them and their families. Yet, as the moment for each of them arrives, they leave with a sense of purpose. Their work in Bolivia is completed, but there is work to be done elsewhere.

Placid Lake Tumi Chucua (left) became the site of the SIL center in Bolivia in 1954. By April 3, 1982, when SIL turned its Amazon jungle education facilities over to the Bolivian Government, SIL linguists had published eight New Testaments. Work is still continuing to finish Scripture translations in four other languages.

La Paz — The "City of Peace" — is the unofficial capital of Bolivia (below left). SIL has retained an office here for government relations purposes, and a guest house for traveling members.

Chipaya men (below) band together to build a dike of dirt and grass to protect their village following a season of unusually hard rains.

Bolivia's Chipaya — Free, At Last!

No one knows when the Chipaya people first hiked onto the barren, cold plateau of Bolivia's altiplano. It seems that rather than bow under the heavy hand of the Spanish conquerors, the Chipayas decided to escape to the "end of the world." It did not matter that the elements on the altiplano were hostile or that little grew in the dusty desert high in the Andes. Here they were free — free from those who would oppress them. Here they built round sod homes with straw roofs. Here individual families led their small herds of sheep and llamas in search of pasture. Here they planted quinoa, a hardy grain — the only crop that would grow in the salty soil of the altiplano. And here they survived with the resolve never to be dominated by outsiders.

But although they were free from outside domination, the Chipayas were, nevertheless, at the mercy of floods, drought, sickness and death. They were, in fact, slaves to the spirits who, they believed, controlled the elements. Since the Chipayas viewed their life on the remote altiplano as precarious at best, they spent their lives trying to appease the spirits.

Through their town ran lines of altars where they performed rituals and sacrificed animals. Their fiestas included a kind of dance marathon in which men and women, accompanied by snatches of music endlessly repeated on flutes, drums and panpipes, danced through freezing nights and long weary days, afraid to stop lest they offend the spirits.

During each major fiesta, every Chipaya family sacrificed a sheep, a llama and a pig. And when there was sickness or some other misfortune, the Chipayas performed repeated sacrifices which often left a family economically devastated.

In 1961, a tall North American and his wife stepped into this world of impersonal spiritual power and hopelessness. Ron and Fran Olson were outsiders, and outsiders were not welcome. However since two other couples had come and gone, the Chipayas were convinced the Olsons would also leave. It seemed safe to offer to build them a house on the condition they make their own doors and windows and bring their own poles and cane for the roof. "Then," the Chipayas said, "you can live in the house for as long as you want."

While the Chipayas believed theirs was the world's original language, they could not understand why the Olsons wanted to learn to speak it. "Unless," they reasoned, "the Olsons want to sell it." It followed then that anyone who helped the Olsons learn the Chipaya language would be a traitor to the tribe.

Thus, when the Olsons first began to probe into the intricate structure of the Chipaya language, the Chipayas deliberately jumbled the sentence structure and gave them incorrect words for the objects the Olsons asked about. Fortunately, several Chipaya men wanted to hear their own voices on tape. They repeated experiences and told folk stories into the Olson's tape recorder. By studying these correctly constructed sentences and stories, the Olsons began to unravel the Chipaya language.

When Ron and Fran first arrived among the Chipayas, there was only one believer, a man named Ceferino. As a youth, Ceferino lived away from his people and learned to speak Spanish and Aymara. When he returned as an adult,

Ceferino attended a meeting sponsored by the Bolivian Indian Mission and there accepted the Lord.

Two years later, the Olsons met Ceferino, and as they became acquainted with him, they learned that he alone refused to take part in ritual sacrifices and drinking. Because of this refusal, the community had ostracized him. The Olsons knew Ceferino would be a great help in learning the Chipaya language, but they decided not to ask for his help because they did not want to turn the community against him.

With almost no language help, Ron and Fran looked for quiet ways to show their love and gain the people's confidence. Ron helped with community projects and repaired bicycles. He made toy cars for the boys by nailing tin can lids onto pieces of wood, and Fran helped little girls and their mothers sew rag dolls.

Occasionally, when the shaman's cures were not successful, the people came to the Olsons for medical help. Ron soon learned the Chipayas thought the shots were bad because they "pierced the body and allowed evil things to enter." But because sulfa and antibiotics worked wonders, the people slowly began to trust him.

It was another matter, however, for the Chipayas to accept the idea of one true God. Sometimes their sacrifices seemed useless, yet they were afraid *not* to sacrifice. They were convinced that health, good crops and large flocks depended upon appeasing the spirits. However, Ceferino's quiet testimony of a good God more powerful than the evil spirits made a few of the Chipayas question the old ways.

One of these was Maximo Felipe. When Maximo's firstborn son became seriously ill with dysentery, he sacrificed two sheep. When the child did not improve, he went to the shaman again and was told that the spirits of his parents were demanding the sacrifice of a white llama; if he did not comply, his child would die. Anger and resentment welled up within him. Both his parents had died when he was a child, leaving him nothing. Maximo thought, "They abandoned me and now they are asking for the life of my child.

They know I don't have the money to buy a white llama!" Angry and depressed, he trudged home.

Later that night Maximo went to Ceferino who encouraged him to talk to Ron. Ron gave Maximo medicine and talked to him about the good God who loved him. With the medicine, his son soon recovered. Grateful for the recovery, Maximo told Ron he had decided to enter God's way, but first he must fulfill his responsibilities as a *muyucama*, one who made sacrifices for the fields that had been planted.

True to his word, after harvest time, Maximo and his wife entered God's way.

Later, Maximo's son became sick again. Maximo and his family were out with their flocks, living in their sod-block home. Their relatives pressured them to go back to the shaman and the old ways.

One night Maximo and his wife watched helplessly as their son, lying in a pile of ragged blankets, gasped for air.

Through her tears, Maximo's wife said, "Maybe God's ways aren't for us. Maybe we should go back to the old ways."

"No," said Maximo, "we've committed ourselves to God. Whether our son lives or dies, we follow the Lord."

With heavy hearts, Maximo and his wife went to sleep, not expecting to see their son alive in the morning. But when they awoke, their son was breathing more easily and on his way to full recovery. The grateful parents never forgot that evidence of God's love and power.

The years passed, and more and more Chipayas began to enter God's way. Ceferino and five or six other men took turns leading the Sunday meetings of worship and Bible study.

As more people left the old ways, the ruling elders became alarmed. Recognizing Ceferino as the leader, they summoned him for questioning and asked him to return to the old ways. When Ceferino told them he could never stop following the true God, they tried to drive him out of town. They also harassed the new believers.

Shortly after this, a measles epidemic swept through the village of Chipaya, killing some adults and almost all the children under two. Out of 800 people, 135 died. Of the believers' families, only Maximo's baby daughter died. In the midst of their grief and confusion, the Chipayas tried to understand what had happened. Was God just protecting the Christians, or had the Christians asked God to punish those who persecuted them? They chose to believe the latter, and their antagonism toward the Christians grew.

As Maximo prepared to bury his little daughter, he was told, "You can't bury her in the cemetery! You're not a Chipaya. You're a Christian. Throw her out! Let the dogs eat her!"

The Lord had walked with Maximo through the shadow of death when his son nearly died, and now in this new crisis, He supplied the needed strength. Rather than retreat or retaliate, Maximo calmly insisted he was both a Chipaya *and* a Christian, and he intended to bury his daughter in the cemetery. Finally, yielding to his quiet determination, they let him bury her in an obscure corner of the cemetery.

The rejection of the Christians and the conviction that they were disrupting the lives of the townspeople persisted. Each year when the communal planting lands were divided, people threatened to withhold land from the Christians. Patiently the Christians stood their ground and each year were finally granted land, though some years it was the very poorest.

As the number of believers increased, so did the antagonism of the unbelievers. One morning a group of believers met in the center of town to sing and listen to a visiting preacher. Enraged, the townspeople hurled stones at them and attacked the preacher. They tore his clothes, beat him, kicked him and dragged him out of town. They scattered the believers, chasing one man several kilometers out of town before they caught him and tore his clothes off.

This was the beginning of a new wave of perse-

43

watched in dismay. They diverted the main streams and sacrificed sheep to appease the angry spirits, but still the rain fell. The rising water washed away all their precious crops and surrounded the town, turning the streets into rivers and the town square into a lake. Their adobe homes began to collapse; their sheep, llamas and pigs were without food.

Frantically, they prayed to all the spirits and sacrificed more animals. For two weeks everything was under water, and they began to fear for their lives. Finally in desperation, the town officials and many others came to the believers begging them to pray to *their* God to see if *He* could stop the rain and save them.

Lightning crackled and thunder rolled as the Chipayas waded through the town to the big church, the largest meeting place in town. After a period of hymn singing, Maximo urged the nonbelievers to abandon their idols and turn to God. "Don't be afraid, because God is going to help us," he said. Then he prayed, "Father God, show your power by stopping the rain and saving us. Show the people that You hear us and that You have power over everything."

The sky remained dark and the rain still fell as the Chipayas waded back to their soggy homes that Sunday afternoon, but by sundown the sky began to clear. That night the stars appeared, and Monday dawned clear. In wonder and relief they watched as day after day the sun shone and the water receded. In a week the town was dry!

Those who had ridiculed the believers were silenced. "Surely you are in touch with God!" they said to the believers. As a result of that "contest," 17 families decided to follow the Lord. Among them was Tomas, one of the powerful

cution. As in Acts, the unbelievers went after the Christians mercilessly. They hunted them down and threatened to destroy their homes, throw them out of town, and confiscate their flocks.

Again tragedy struck: unexpected freezes killed many of the unbelievers' quinoa plants. They saw this as God's judgment on them and reluctantly dropped their threats.

A few more years slipped by. Ron and Fran steadily translated the New Testament and taught people to read. Primers, Bible stories and songbooks were completed.

Then, in 1974, God showed His power in a manner reminiscent of the days of Elijah and the contest on Mount Carmel, except that instead of *no* rain, there was *too much* rain.

As the rain fell, the rivers rose. The Chipayas

shamans who had opposed the Olsons and other believers.

As respect for the believers grew, the persecution stopped. Gradually they were given positions of leadership in the community — at first minor responsibilities, then more important roles.

As more Chipayas chose to follow Christ, fewer and fewer remained to make the large number of sacrifices. Every idol and spirit-place required at least one animal sacrifice a year; many required three or even more. The load became so heavy that several times the caretakers of shrines asked the believers to destroy the shrines!

In 1977 the completion of the New Testament drew near. The Olsons, planning a much needed furlough, determined to complete the New Testament before leaving.

Dedication Day was set for Easter Sunday, 1978 — eight months away. That meant in eight months the manuscript would have to be rechecked, retyped, printed and bound. It seemed humanly impossible.

But, in spite of setbacks, the work moved ahead. Maximo was consistently available to help with the checking. An extra typist came from the United States. The printing press broke down but was soon repaired. The folding machine wrinkled the pages, forcing the Olsons and others to fold everything by hand. The plane that was to fly the Olsons and the New Testaments to Chipaya developed engine trouble that had the pilot-mechanics baffled for days. Yet in spite of it all, the New Testaments were printed and delivered on time.

The dedication was a triumphant celebration.

Two hundred and fifty Chipaya believers marched through town singing of God's love. In one way or another, the entire Chipaya church participated in the dedication service. Some spoke, telling how faithful God had been to them. Others, accompanied by violin, accordian and guitar, sang special songs. Others served the noon meal to the entire community.

Finally Maximo closed the all-day celebration with a prayer of praise and thanksgiving to God, at the same time rededicating his life for service to God.

A few weeks later the Olsons left for furlough, praying that the 70 New Testaments in the hands of the believers would strengthen and encourage them to reach out to their neighbors. In remarkable ways, the prayers of the Olsons, of their many friends and supporters, and of the Chipayas themselves were realized. Five years later, most of the Chipayas were professing Christians.

Thus the Chipayas have found freedom, not by escaping as they once did, but by following the Lord. They are free from the old fears and domination of the spirits; free to serve a powerful and loving God!

John 8:36 in Chipaya

Jalla niżtiquiztan ančhucqui Yooz majchiż liwriita cjequiż niique ultim werara liwriita cjequičha, Yooz kjuychiz famillquiz cjisjapaqui.

"So if the Son sets you free, you will be free indeed."

45

NORTH AMERICA

In 1663, Puritan clergyman John Elliot published the Massachusetts Indian Bible — the first translation of Scriptures into a North American Indian language. That language was known for its long complex words, the longest in that Bible being "Watappe-sittukqussunnoohwehtunkguoh." Found in Mark 1:40, it means "kneeling down to Him." Although the Massachusetts Indian language is no longer spoken and its Bible is a museum piece, the translation was a significant 17th Century recognition of the Church's responsibility to make God's Word available to all people in the language they understand best.

Today, WBT and SIL help carry on the translation task in North America. More than 100 translators, linguists and support personnel serve 40 language groups in Canada and the U.S. In addition, there are two home divisions in the Area — the Canada Division with its headquarters in Alberta, and the U.S. Division with its headquarters in California.

The North America Branch covers a larger geographic area than any other SIL field operation, stretching from the swamps of Florida to windy St. Lawrence Island off the coast of Siberia, and from the far reaches of northeastern Quebec to the coastal mountains of Southern California.

The diversity of language projects underway is striking. In addition to Indian and Eskimo groups, SIL is working with a group of English-based Creole speakers and several groups from other countries, such as the Tai Dam refugees from Vietnam who now live in Iowa.

Of the 40 language groups with whom SIL has worked, five have received translated New Testaments: the Navajo, Western Apache, Hopi and Papago Indians and the Inupiat Eskimos. Several other New Testaments are nearing completion and many other groups have Scripture portions, as well as dictionaries and other literacy materials.

An important objective of the work in North America is the ever-increasing involvement of the native peoples in the Bible translation process, as shown by the Crow and Cree language projects described in the following section.

Bible translation is still needed in North America. Some may have overlooked these groups, but God has not. He still wants them to have His Word in their own languages. And, one by one, He is making it happen.

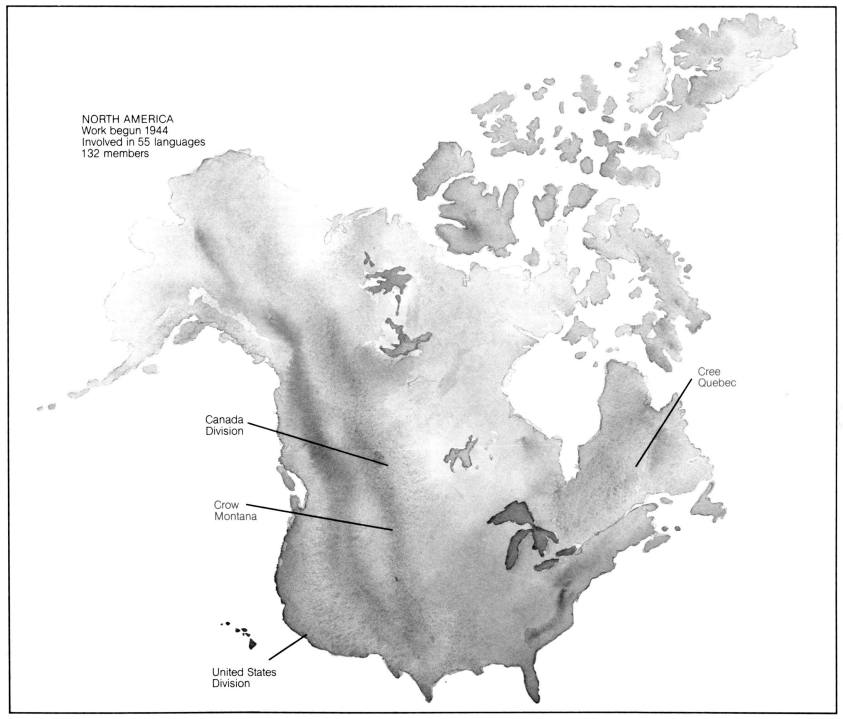

NORTH AMERICA
Work begun 1944
Involved in 55 languages
132 members

Cree
Quebec

Canada
Division

Crow
Montana

United States
Division

His Eye is on the Crow, Too

W hile I was fasting, 'Firstmaker' came to me," said Chief Plenty Coups, last of the Crow Indian chiefs. "I saw the buffalo being swallowed up by the prairie. In their stead came many, many smaller brown animals and a multitude of people with pale skin. I then saw a tree bending with the wind but not breaking. Then my vision ended."

The assembled council of Crow elders, to whom Plenty Coups was repeating this vision, reportedly interpreted his vision as symbolizing the coming of the white man and cattle. They believed the bending tree was a warning for them to work with the white man rather than resist and be broken.

In any case, relationships between the Crows and the white man have been relatively peaceful down through the years. In fact, if General Custer had listened to the warnings of his Crow scouts, he would never have fought the famous Battle of the Little Big Horn, in which he and his men were massacred.

Who are these Crow people who made such a wise decision about their future destiny?

The ancestors of the present-day Crows came to North America with speakers of other languages in the Siouan family. When the white man first encountered the Crows, they were living south of Lake Superior. Population pressures forced them to move southward and westward. The arrival of the horse in the Plains Indian culture brought a new and greatly increased mobility and wealth. The increased mobility also brought all the Plains tribes into contact and often into conflict with each other. The Crow re-

Warfare with the Cheyennes, Blackfeet and Sioux made the Crow a hardy and brave people. Today the Crow celebrate their heritage in special Indian Day festivities that include dances accompanied by drums, special food and beautiful buckskin clothing (left).

(Below) The Crow Indian Reservation today is only a fraction of the size of their original land base. An area about the size of Delaware, it is comprised of 2,300 square miles of rolling grasslands and low, forested mountain ranges. Game and fish abound on the reservation, as do natural resources: timber, grazing lands, coal and water.

Jeanne Miska and daughter Sarah enjoy a special morning ride (bottom).

sponded by moving still further westward to the Rockies, where there were fewer tribal groups.

Religion has always been important to the Crows. They have felt dependent for their survival and success on cooperation with, and guidance from, the spirit world. Like other Plains groups, their religious life has featured rituals for specific occasions, annual ceremonies such as their Sun Dance (which continues today) and the "vision quest." In the latter, a person goes to a lonely place and fasts until he receives a vision which, when interpreted, gives him direction and often some specific benefit.

Just about the time the Crow Reservation was established in the 1880's, the Jesuits began mission work among the Crows. In 1901, at the invitation of some of the people, the American Baptist Convention began a work on the reservation. Later an indigenous Pentecostal church became a strong factor in the religious life of the people.

By and large, the Crow people were open to God's Good News, and many of them "followed the Jesus road," as they called their new Christian life. In the early 1920s, revival broke out on the reservation, and the Christian groups grew strong.

Although most of the early missionaries learned to speak the Crow language, none of them took the steps necessary to produce the Scriptures in Crow — the language the people understood best. While government and mission schools trained the people to use the English language, most of the Crow people remained unable to fully appreciate and comprehend biblical teaching.

Then God began to lay His hand on those He had chosen to translate the Scriptures into the Crows' heart language.

Jerome Hugs was one of these. When Jerome was a boy, a woman living in his hometown of Pryor, Montana, offered him and his friends a ride. As they drove, the woman witnessed to them. Silently Jerome prayed for salvation but never revealed his interest or his decision.

Later, as a teenager, Jerome became involved in activities that drew his interest away from spiritual things, but often he would feel God's tug on his heart. He would hear an evangelist on his car radio when he least expected it, or a Gospel tract saying, "God wants you!" would arrive mysteriously in the mail. Little prayers would be answered. Every time Jerome saw a Bible, he would say to himself, "Not now. Later."

His wife and daughters became Christians and began to pray for him, but as his inner struggle became more intense, he argued with them more and more. A recurring theme in his arguments was Indian religion and its relationship to Christianity. "I was trying to hang onto my Indian identity," Jerome said later. "I didn't know the Lord just wanted to make me a better Indian."

It was in March of 1974 that Jerome turned his life over to the Lord. The same month the Lord led Fred and Jeanne Miska to commit themselves to Bible translation among Jerome's people. The Miskas went to Montana with the strong conviction that God wanted a good, communicative Bible translation for the Crows. Furthermore, they believed this would be more likely to happen if a native speaker of the Crow language became heavily involved in the translation process.

After meeting Jerome, the Miskas believed Jerome was the Crow-speaker God had chosen for translation work. However, when Jerome learned why the Miskas had come to the reservation, he said, "What will the white man think of next! What use is there for the Bible in the Crow tongue?"

Assured that Jerome was indeed God's choice, Fred spent time with Jerome, discipling him and sharing everyday activities. Together they picked berries, rode horseback and cut logs. Fred often prayed with Jerome and answered his questions

Throughout their work among the Crow, translators Fred and Jeanne Miska have encouraged the believers to assume responsibility for the translation. From this has emerged an enthusiastic translation committee which works hand in glove with the Miskas (below). Others, like computer operator and secretary Pat Moffett, have worked with the committee as short term assistants (right).

Through a bilingual education program, more and more school materials like this reading book (below) are becoming available in Crow.

about relating his new understanding of Jesus Christ to his old life. Rather than giving his opinions, Fred wisely pointed Jerome to the Scriptures.

Fred also shared with Jerome his conviction that God was calling Jerome to Bible translation work. Eventually Jerome came to share that conviction and began to work with Fred on translation. As Jerome worked with the Scriptures, they became more precious and meaningful to him. "At first I didn't think the Bible in Crow was very important," said Jerome. "But now I can see it's in God's plan. Now translation is my life!"

Jerome is now head translator, with primary responsibility for the quality and accuracy of the translation. He is assisted by other Crow-speakers who review his work or serve as resource persons. Fred serves as exegetical consultant and project facilitator. An auxiliary Crow-speaking translation unit works in Lodge Grass, Montana, a hundred miles east of Pryor. Short-term assistant Pat Moffett serves everyone as secretary. She is also the computer keyboard operator, but is training a Crow woman to take over this responsibility.

The committee giving general oversight to the team's work consists of five non-Indians, a Hopi Indian, and nine Crow Indians who represent the Crow religious and linguistic communities.

There's more to the story than successful teambuilding. The churches are beginning to look forward to receiving newly-translated portions. The team members use the translated Scriptures in visits to alcoholism treatment centers, old age homes and jails, as well as on a regular radio program.

The people are finding that the Scriptures speak to their life problems. For example, political strife and division on the reservation had resulted in the impeachment of three consecutive tribal chairmen. When the team translated chapter two of I Timothy, the members were challenged by Paul's exhortation to pray for their leaders.

The translation team shared the Scripture passage throughout the reservation — from the pulpit, in visits to homes, over the radio — and urged the Crow Christians to pray for their tribal leaders. The people responded. Meeting in small groups, they began to pray in earnest that their leaders might have wisdom and that Christianity might grow and prosper on the reservation.

As one possible result, a political meeting was interrupted one afternoon so that everyone could listen to the translation team's radio broadcast.

The translated Scriptures have influenced individual lives, too. A woman and her son both made a commitment to Christ after listening to a tape of Acts in their home. Commenting on the clarity and vividness of the translation, one Crow man said, "It's just like watching a movie!"

The Crow team members, convinced of the value of the Scriptures in their own language, have carried their vision for Bible translation to other tribes. They have made visits to the Paiute, Blackfoot, Western Cree, Stoney, Beaver and other groups. They are also making plans to start a training center on their reservation where they can share with other Indian translators what they have learned.

The Miskas marvel as they contemplate what God has done for the Crow people. Said Fred, "All the men on the Crow translation team were once non-Christians and alcoholics. None of them had any formal education beyond high school nor had they been to Bible school. None of them could read or write the Crow language.

"Now all the men have turned their lives over to Christ and maintain a close walk with God. I encourage their faith, and they do the same for me. They even exhort me when I need it. I'm constantly being broadened by their understanding of the Word as they translate. God has taken their informal training and multiplied it so His Word can become available in the Crow language. The exciting thing about having this team involvement is that the end-product is superior to what it would have been if Jeanne and I were the translators and the Crows merely helped us do our work."

The reality of this fact came home to Fred one day when he asked Jerome, "What would you do if we suddenly had to leave the translation work?"

Jerome's answer was one every SIL translator would like to hear from mother-tongue translation colleagues. Said Jerome, "I'd just go on translating."

53

Partnership in Cree Translation

To hear a recital of Canadian Indian band names is to experience a rhythm reminiscent of the rumble of distant drums. Names like Ojibway, Chipewyan, Huron, Iroquois, Algonquin, Salish, Blackfoot, Mohawk, Mistassini Cree, Micmac, Beaver, Dogrib, Sarcee, and more. On and on they go — noble names, proud names that resound in the mind like an epic poem or a grand opera, both beautiful and tragic.

Stretching from British Columbia and the Yukon in the west, across the Northwest Territories and the windswept prairies to the eastern Newfoundland seaboard, Indian nations have enriched Canada and the world with resplendent place names, unique languages and traditional cultures.

One such Indian band is the Mistassini Cree of northern Quebec. The 2,000 Mistassini Crees belong to the Eastern Cree nation, a group of 7,000 people who live in eight villages scattered over an area of 400 square miles. Skillful hunters, trappers and woodsmen, the Mistassini Cree have for generations made their home around the deep and beautiful Lake Mistassini and in the village of the same name.

Although their part in history has been underplayed, the Cree people, like many other Indian bands, played a strategic role in the foundation and development of the Dominion of Canada. Early in the 19th century, furs were in high demand. French and Indian trappers alike scrambled to make their fortunes. This highly lucrative enterprise made the city of Montreal Canada's chief financial and power center.

It was the Cree and other Indian peoples who knew intimately where the finest furs were to be found. They also knew best how to trap, skin and tan the hides for the large mercantile companies. Like the French voyageurs, they traveled down the great rivers of the northern watershed to James Bay, Rupert's House, Moose Factory and other famous trading posts to sell and trade their furs. And like their southern cousins in the United States, the Indian fur trappers fell victim to lawless men who filled them with liquor, cheated them of their furs and settled their quarrels with gun and knife.

All those events happened less than 200 years ago. With the passage of time, the fur trade in Quebec diminished as a major industry. In its place came lumbering, mining, agriculture, manufacturing and other industries. In the rush to establish their economic kingdoms, the descen-

Rodney Bartlett and co-translator Louise Blacksmith confer on a Scripture passage for the Mistassini Cree (left below).

(Left) Typical of Cree design, this snowshoe is almost circular.

The Cree practice a semi-nomadic life-style of hunting, fishing and trapping which reflects their close proximity to the land. During their four to six months in the bush, whole families live out the harsh northern Quebec winters in canvas tents (below).

Weather dulls the sign on the Band Council Office (right). The elected members of the Band Council provide a liaison between the Federal and provincial governments, and the Cree.

The Mistassini Cree belong to the Eastern Cree nation whose 7,000 people live in eight villages that cover over 400 square miles of rivers, forests, marshes and wetlands (below right).

dents of the early French Canadians and British settlers were for the most part indifferent to Indian values, needs and culture.

Like other Indian bands, the Mistassini Cree have struggled to survive as a unique people in a world that always seems to be overpowering them. Yet, perhaps because of their geographical isolation, the retention of their language, and their determination to keep what is most mean-ingful in their culture, the Mistassini Cree have won the right to live and work and die as Indians.

One of the special characteristics the Cree have retained is their semi-nomadic life-style. With canoes, fishing nets, rifles, trapping gear, canvas tents, spruce-bough floors, airtight stoves and other equipment, families — sometimes including grandparents — live and hunt in comfortable harmony with nature during the harsh winters and springs of northern Quebec.

While living and hunting in the bush is perhaps the single most important activity in the lives of the Mistassini Cree, there is yet another practice that celebrates their Indianness almost as much as their nomadic life-style. It is the use of old decorative Indian symbols — triangles, arches, wedges, pothooks and fishhooks — to write their Cree language.

More than a century ago, James Evans, an English missionary working with the Western Cree around Hudson Bay, longed for the Cree to be able to read the Scriptures in their own language. In his day, the science of descriptive linguistics was virtually unknown. Yet without the aid of modern linguistic tools, Evans studied the phonological patterns of the Cree language and created a syllabary — a writing system based on syllables rather than individual letters. Each symbol of the syllabary represented a Cree sound or vowel-consonant combination.

It is unclear how Evans first decided to incorporate the distinctive Indian shapes into his syllabary. Some believe he copied the decorative patterns the Cree worked into their mooseskin jackets and backpacks. However he made that decision, Evans struck a deep emotional core in the Cree when he used this perfect blending of familiar elements with artistic meaning to teach something completely unknown.

While the syllabary has been and is being used among the Cree, and while it is accepted by the people (particularly the older people) as part of their Indian tradition, it remains a painful ordeal to read. This is particularly true for longer passages, which means that its usefulness for instruction and enjoyment is limited.

Because of this difficulty and because the only Scripture translation available to the Cree was in another dialect called Moose Cree, the Anglican minister in Mistassini asked that an SIL team provide a translation for the Eastern Cree believers. In 1973, Canadian Rodney Bartlett, and his German-born wife, Liesel, began an exciting adventure into the Cree language and culture. Like all beginning translators, the Bartletts made their share of cultural and language blunders. Rodney once wrote, "Language learning is both fun and a struggle. Sometimes it can even be embarrassing. Once we managed to swear at the Indians instead of asking, 'Are you trapping?' On another occasion I asked, 'How is your old man?' instead of, 'How are you feeling?'"

Rodney and Liesel learned from their mistakes and, in their earlier years in the community, enjoyed extended periods of time with Cree families in their winter hunting camps. They shared the Cree life-style and learned the Cree language and culture. Such exposure better equipped them to work on Scripture translation, make

With their children, Rodney and Liesel take a break from the translation desk for a spring walk outside their home at Mistassini Lake (far left).

The Cree syllabary, seen on Cree gravestones (left), is still a meaningful part of Cree tradition.

(Below) The village of Mistassini has three churches to serve approximately 2,000 people. In all three churches there is high interest in the use of the translated Cree Scriptures.

Liesel (with daughter Heather on her lap) works with Clara Cooper who, like other Cree believers, has assumed responsibility to check for readability, style and grammatical correctness in the Cree New Testament (below).

OVERLEAF: To learn more about the Cree language and culture, Rod and Liesel spent their first winter of their Cree assignment living with a family in the bush.

primers and record Cree crafts in storybooks.

The Bartletts have discovered that, while the new Roman alphabet they are using is easier to read than the old syllabic symbols, some of the older Cree still prefer the syllabary. For this reason, they plan to print the Eastern Cree New Testament in both the Roman alphabet and the symbols of the syllabary.

To the first time observer, the Bartlett life-style seems extremely casual. Children of all ages scamper in and out of the house. People drop in unannounced. The kettle on the wood-burning stove is ever ready for a pot of tea.

Nevertheless, in the midst of the happy clutter of activity, a team of people is translating God's Word and readying what has been translated for distribution.

At a handsome jackpine table in the kitchen, Rodney Bartlett works out the exegesis of the text. He pays special attention to figures of speech, such as hyperbole and metaphor. Once he understands the passage, he writes a rough draft in Cree. He frequently confers with his co-translator, Cree-speaker Louise Blacksmith, to make sure that the expressions he uses will be understood. The Crees, for example, use the compound word *flour-bush* to refer to *wheat*. On one occasion Louise suggested the Crees would understand the concept of *wilderness* if they used *the place where nothing grows*.

When Rodney feels satisfied with his rough draft, he feeds his material into what has become a mini-assembly line. In a corner of the wide hall between the kitchen and living room, Cree-speaker Clara Cooper works with Liesel Bartlett. Clara and Liesel go over Rodney's draft verse by verse. When they are comfortable that the verses communicate the correct meaning, Clara types them on a battered black portable typewriter.

Clara takes the translated materials to Louise, who works in a room off the kitchen. She proofreads the text and keyboards it into a computer.

Five days a week, six to seven hours a day, Louise and Clara work at their respective areas of translation. Others, like Beatrice and Charlie Petawabono and Harry Meskino, regularly check the translation for naturalness and accuracy. The three Mistassini churches are so committed to the completion of the Cree Bible translation project that they regularly contribute funds toward it.

Sometimes the Bartletts take contracts from the

Consultant Jonathan Ekstrom (left center) leads a translation workshop handling grammatical patterns, vocabulary and cultural adjustments.

Leisel's breath forms frost on her eyelashes and hair (center). In the intense cold of a Quebec winter, nose hairs freeze when inhaling and thaw when exhaling.

The Bartletts make periodic visits to the bush where many Cree families prefer to spend their winters (below).

Cree school board's adult education department to develop materials for a Cree reading program.

As if these tasks were not enough to keep the team occupied, the Anglican minister regularly requests printouts of each week's translated materials to be used in the evening service. "We are pleased to provide this for the churches," says Rodney. "Our little computer printer is not built to handle forty copies of a book that may run ten pages long. Nevertheless, we do it with joy, knowing that the translated Scriptures are being used throughout the churches in Mistassini. This, after all, is what the Cree translation team is all about."

Liesel Bartlett recalls the time when she became aware that God was leading her toward Bible translation. "As I understood how important the Word of God was to my own personal spiritual development, I was impressed that, among the many language groups on earth, there were still so many who didn't have the Scriptures in their own language.

"I was aware that a superabundance of Scripture commentaries and helps was available to me in my own German language, while almost nothing was available for many people on earth. I found myself blaming the Lord for not providing the Scriptures for the people who didn't have them. But one day in the middle of my prayers, the Lord faced me with my own question and asked, 'WHAT COULD YOU DO ABOUT IT?' Later, as I searched the Scriptures, the Lord impressed upon me the necessity of going to help, and that's all I needed!"

ASIA

Nestled in the mountain regions of the Philippines, Ifugao believers read from well-used copies of the New Testament recently completed by a Canadian translator with their help. Two thousand miles away, Indonesian young people, eager to translate Scriptures for their own people, listen attentively to a lecture on translation principles.

These two situations illustrate the variety of approaches being used to reach the diverse peoples of Asia. In some cases, SIL workers live and work among the people for whom they are translating. In other cases, SIL is training national translators to work among their own people or among other minority groups within their homeland. Translations for still other groups are being done outside of Asia with the aid of people who have emigrated from their homeland. Where published Scripture cannot be distributed, radio programs of Scripture reading are reaching the people.

Twenty-two countries come under the responsibility of the Asia Area director — 20 of these with active programs. The area contains over one-half the world's population and one-third of its languages. While work is underway in some 150 languages, the translation needs for more than 700 others must still be determined.

An increasing number of Asians are joining the more than 600 workers in the Asia Area. Interest in Bible translation is growing and Wycliffe home offices have been established in Japan, Korea and Singapore. There are now nearly 40 SIL team members from seven Asian nations.

At times the task in Asia seems overwhelming. Yet, in spite of its enormity and complexity, progress is being made. God is providing the people and the guidance needed to complete the job.

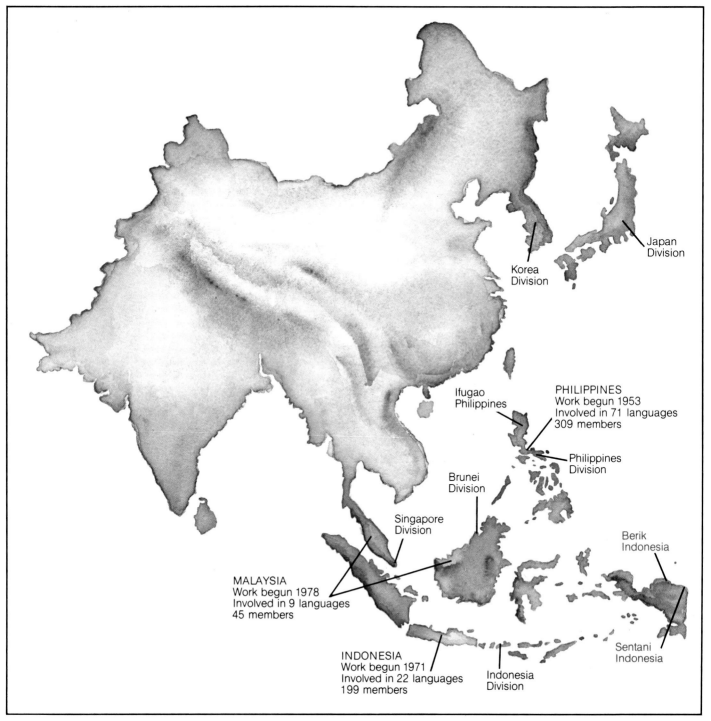

Korea
Division

Japan
Division

Ifugao
Philippines

PHILIPPINES
Work begun 1953
Involved in 71 languages
309 members

Philippines
Division

Brunei
Division

Singapore
Division

Berik
Indonesia

MALAYSIA
Work begun 1978
Involved in 9 languages
45 members

INDONESIA
Work begun 1971
Involved in 22 languages
199 members

Indonesia
Division

Sentani
Indonesia

Indonesia —
Unity In Diversity

L ike a widely scattered jigsaw puzzle, the islands of the Indonesian archipelago stretch in a huge crescent from Asia to Australia. Straddling the equator, Indonesia stretches from east to west over a distance greater than the distance between Los Angeles and New York. Its islands number more than 13,000, some no bigger than a small reef, but others, such as Java, large enough to support a population of 90 million people.

For 300 years the Dutch, with their monolithic East India Company, controlled these islands and their waterways. The Japanese invasion of 1941, however, destroyed colonialism in southeast Asia. Then on August 17, 1945, just two days after the surrender of Japan, Indonesian nationalists in Jakarta, the capital city, proclaimed independence. The Republic of Indonesia was born.

Since independence, the Indonesia government has striven to promote unity in diversity through the outworking of the five guiding principles of the republic. Called the *Panca Sila*, the principles are: 1) belief in one supreme God, 2) a just and civilized (developed) humanity, 3) the building of nationhood through a common language, 4) the participation of all in the political process, and 5) social justice.

SIL members, of course, also believe in one Supreme God. In addition, SIL is committed to sharing its scientific and practical knowledge with those seeking to benefit and upgrade a given community. It was for these reasons that national planners first became interested in the work of the Summer Institute of Linguistics. They felt that SIL's three-fold program of scientific language analysis, community development (including the advancement of literacy), and the translation of the Scriptures into the local languages would further the goals of the *Panca Sila*.

Thus in 1971, SIL signed a contract with the University of Indonesia, and SIL members officially entered the country. A year later SIL was invited to work with the Cenderawasih University of Abepura, Irian Jaya, and contracts have since been signed with that university which have broadened the scope of cooperation between the two entities.

Agreements have recently been signed to work in the Maluku Islands (once known as the Spice Islands) and in Sulawesi.

Dick Hugoniot, SIL's director in Indonesia, states, "We have a strong partnership with the university, including teaching involvement. We are involved in community development, and both expatriates and nationals are translating the Scriptures.

"Churches are being born out of the translation process and existing churches, for many years without the Scriptures, are now receiving the translated Word and are growing and being encouraged and enriched."

Clouds, gleaming white, billow around Lake Sentani in Irian Jaya. Home of 16,000 Sentani people, this beautiful tropical lake stretches for 25 miles around the base of the Cyclops Mountains.

One Translator's Early Impressions

Margaret Hartzler, translator with her husband Dwight to the Sentani of Indonesia, recounts experiences of their early days.

It's our language! It's our language!" shouted the old lady above the jostling crowd. Dressed in her market best, the woman pulled a book out of Dwight Hartzler's hands. Curious onlookers gathered around. The woman called again, "It's our language!" and the Sentanis in the crowd moved toward her.

"Has our language been written down?" asked a curious onlooker. Then as if to answer the question, a man began to read aloud. The crowd murmured, "It's true! This book is not in Bahasa Indonesia. It is in our own mother tongue and it is telling us about the life of Jesus."

Later, when Dwight arrived home, he greeted me with a big smile. "Fifty books distributed yesterday and today," he said. "I traded some for vegetables and fruit, and one man offered me a stone axe."

This was great news. It had not been too long since we had wondered if the Sentanis would *ever* be interested in learning to read their language.

Lake Sentani, the home of the Sentani people of Irian Jaya, stretches like a 25-mile-long giant crab around the base of the towering Cyclops Mountains. Its inlets and islands, placid in the tropical heat, are home to about 10,000 people in tin or sago-stem houses built on stilts over the water. They are fishermen who harvest the lake in canoes, using lines or nets and spears. Sago trees line the shore, and sleeping crocodiles soak in the sun's rays. Grass-covered hills, occasionally

64

crowned by a house or school, rise like sleeping dinosaurs above the trees. The life of a Sentani is a quiet, slow life centered on family and clan activities, the gathering of sago and fish, the tending of gardens.

I remember the day we moved into our house on the island of Ifar Besar. The people ambled along the island path, stepping over weeds and around mudholes, laughing and talking on their way to visit us. High spirited and outgoing, they enjoy the special occasions in their lives, the feasting and the dancing. To them, our arrival was an important event. They had come to see our house, run the water in the bathroom, look at our magazines and wonder at the painting I had hung on the wall. They tested the mattresses, examined my dress, talked for awhile and then went home. They were never pushy, and as the weeks went by, they usually rowed by our front porch and viewed us from a distance, not coming in unless we called out an invitation.

Before we moved in, nearby store owners had warned us not to live there. "You'll be robbed!" they said, but we were not robbed, and the days drifted slowly by until the warnings about being robbed left our minds.

One morning we arose to find a Sentani man at our door who was from a village on the far side of the lake. This was the first time we had met him, and his question was an enigma. Did we know who had stolen his fishing net last night? No we didn't. But why had he come to us? The man's expression implied that we should know. We had a mirror, didn't we? All we had to do was look in it and we could tell him who took his net.

Our protestations fell on deaf ears, and he went away with his own conclusions. Our conclusions

65

were a little more muddled, and Dwight thought he had better discuss the situation with the village chief. Clearly, there was more here than met the eye.

When Dwight arrived home after visiting the chief, he had his answer. In order to protect us from thieves, the chief had told his people we could look into our mirror and know who had stolen our possessions. It was a great story, and everyone believed it because it was consistent with traditional Sentani beliefs. Some families have little bags that knock when someone in the family dies, so why not a looking glass that reveals thieves? It was wonderfully effective, too — until the first time we left the village for an extended period. We returned later to find that the contents of our house had been rifled and every mirror broken.

Over the years, the Sentanis have been exposed to other cultures and values, yet they have been able to cling to their own lifestyle. Hearing and responding to the Christian message over the past 50 years has not changed their basic lifestyle. Nor has adopting Western dress and attending Indonesian schools.

The Sentanis saw the Japanese come in 1942 and watched as bombs fell from the skies. With the American invasion of 1944, they saw the Japanese leave. They enjoyed leftover U.S. food rations, and some even learned to sing cowboy songs.

When the Americans left, the Sentanis used the cast-off tin to fix their houses and moved the Quonset huts into their favorite position — over the lake. Life continued as before. Their views of who God is and their relationship to Him were changing, but their language, their clan system

and many basic sets of rules that governed their lives remained intact. Their continuing satisfaction with their traditional lifestyle was reflected in their daily activities: fishing, eating sago and enjoying the quiet black nights and the soft sound of lapping water around their homes on Lake Sentani.

This contentment with their own culture and life-style worked in two ways for us. On the one hand they were reluctant to break their traditional patterns of living long enough to help us prepare and check books. We were reminded

they still had to pound their sago and catch fish. Clan meetings had to be attended, and they needed to campaign to put a Sentani in the provincial assembly.

On the other hand, the thought that someone outside their own group was concerned enough to try to learn their language was attractive. Their longtime interest in carving designs on their boats, houses and drums led naturally to the idea of writing in their language. In all the years we have known the Sentani people, only one felt need has ever been expressed to us — the need to

Usiel Pallo and the Hartzlers (below) have translated the Gospel of Luke, Acts, a Life of Christ booklet and numerous hymns for the Sentani church.

While a group of Sentani women wait to catch a canoe ride back to their islands, a Javanese market woman sells them a snack of savory Indonesian fritters (right).

With approximately 800 distinct languages and dialects spoken in the Indonesian archipelago, this woman (far right) smiles with delight when she is shown a book (the Life of Christ) translated into the Sentani language.

have their language written and to see the Word of God printed in their own language. It was the open expression of this need that first attracted us to the Sentanis.

On their own the Sentanis have translated songs and given them to us to print. With joy they sing all these songs in the language they love.

"It's our language!" "Aei afaeunge!" In my mind I hear those words again and see their awestruck faces. God has spoken to His people! This time it is in Sentani.

Community Service: Government Leaders' Training Course

T
he rains had broken and the clouds were clearing as the Helio Courier climbed into the sky over the Sentani airport. On board were six Indonesian leaders who were developing a program for placing government workers in rural districts of Irian Jaya. These workers would need to know how to relate to different cultures, how to defeat boredom in isolated jungle settlements and how to cope with their environment. The men charged with developing the program had asked the Summer Institute of Linguistics for help, and the men were now on their way to Danau Bira, SIL's jungle study center, for a week of intensive study in cross-cultural understanding.

When the plane touched down and stopped on the rain-soaked grass airstrip, Pete Silzer, the SIL course leader for the week, warmly welcomed the men. Pete had long been interested in introducing Indonesian citizens to SIL's goals of linguistic and cultural research, Scripture translation and literacy work.

Each man who had come was a leader in his own field. One was in charge of developing new programs for his branch of the government. Another was the leader of a government academy. A third was responsible for community relations, and yet another was a medical doctor.

Pete and his assistant, Indonesian Nontje Pattipeiluhu, took the men through a series of lectures about the complex sound and grammar systems of Irian languages and the unique cultures of the people who spoke them. They described the complex verbs of Irian languages. In some of these languages, the verbs include information about the size of the verb's object, the

Sporting the dried windpipe of a cassowary bird on the end of her nonconformist safety pin earring, this Bauzi woman (left) reflects the uniqueness of her own individuality.

One Bauzi village near the SIL center provides a view of how life has been going on for centuries.

In about the time it takes to read this, a Bauzi man is able to produce fire from

friction alone (below). Looping a pencil-thick jungle vine around two balsa sticks that have been padded underneath with tinder, he secures the sticks with his feet and vigorously

seesaws the vine back and forth. Moments later, when a curl of smoke begins to appear, the firemaker carefully blows the spark into a flame.

gender of the speaker, the distance of the speaker from the place of action, the height of objects and the general time of day, as well as tense and negation. Other languages are tonal, with the meanings of words changing depending upon the rise and fall of the speaker's voice.

The six leaders paid special attention to the language spoken in the area around the center — Bauzi. They tried to talk to the people using Bauzi-Indonesian-English conversation books compiled by SIL linguist-translators Dave and Joyce Briley. The men were amazed to find that Bauzi, spoken by a group of 200 semi-nomadic jungle dwellers, had more sounds than the national language. They struggled to pro-

nounce words like *fako* (eye), in which the *k* sounds like it comes from half way down the throat. They spent half a day trying to learn how Bauzi sentences are constructed, finally discovering a very rigid word order quite unlike their own languages. They also learned about cultural differences, such as the exchange rules for marriage: when a Bauzi man wants to marry, he must produce a sister or cousin who can marry into the clan of his future wife.

Sitting cross-legged on the bark floor of a smoke-filled house eating roasted sweet potatoes, the men began to feel the differences of village life. Away from their families and all that was familiar, unable to communicate, these leaders

felt the pressures and alienation their trainees would soon face. They began to realize that language is the key to understanding culture, and cultural understanding the key to good community relations.

In an attempt to show how indiscriminate change from the outside can often be less than beneficial to ethnic communities, Pete told the men one of his own experiences. While living with the Ambai people on Yapen Island, just north of Irian Jaya, Pete had been bothered by the way the people used crudely carved wooden goggles for spearfishing. Although they were adept at their craft, Pete felt they would be even better if they had factory-made rubber goggles. One day 71

Many of the Ambai people, among whom Peter and Sheryl Silzer work, use their expert diving skills to secure food (below). The Ambai are a sophisticated seafaring people who live along the shores of the Island of

Yapan, building their villages on stilts out over the water. Many are educated and a number are studying at Cenderawasih University, with which SIL has a cooperative program.

he bought a few pairs and presented them to his friends. He was invited along when these "new inventions" were tested.

"As we donned our new goggles," said Pete, "all seemed well. We started under water with great expectations of a good catch. Only a few glorious moments passed, however, before one of my friends shot up out of the water and ripped off the new goggles. Not only had they leaked but they had made him see double. How would he know which fish to spear? Replacing the rubber goggles with his old home-made ones, my friend disappeared back into the water and caught his usual quota of fish!"

When the week ended, the six men flew out of Danau Bira with a new understanding and acceptance of their multi-faceted society. They left also with a greater appreciation for SIL. One official remarked at the closing ceremony, "Now I understand why SIL has come to our country."

Cross-Cultural Communications Course

Three Indonesian young people—Usiel Pallo, Sonja Rehatta and Jacob Bemey—all from different worlds but with identical goals: to see God's Word translated into the unwritten languages of Indonesia, and to see people from those language groups reading and writing, and enjoying it.

To achieve these goals, all three attended courses given by the Summer Institute of Linguistics on communicating in a cross-cultural context. A new world of linguistic analysis was opened to them. They learned how to teach people to read and how to accurately translate literature from one language to another. They also studied anthropology and English. "It was very good," says Sentani-speaker Usiel Pallo, his eyes sparkling. "Three of my friends have also taken the course, and they can now help me in my work."

Usiel was born on the island of Ifar Besar in Irian Jaya's beautiful Lake Sentani. Born into a traditional Sentani world, he weeded his gardens, dived for fish, chopped up sago trees for food, and bantered with the boys. Occasionally he hunted wild pig or carved out a canoe. In due time he married.

Usiel did all these traditional things, and more. For six years of elementary school and three years of high school, he rose each morning and rowed his canoe from his island home to the mainland. Then he walked another two miles along the rutted and weed-lined path that led from the lake into the town of Sentani.

Schooling, especially reading, was important to Usiel. "If I don't read every day," says Usiel, "I don't feel good. I want to expand my knowledge.

I like to read everything. Some nights I read my Bible for so long my wife thinks I'm crazy."

When Usiel was young, he dreamed of becoming a pilot. Because he lived close to the Sentani airport and the Mission Aviation Fellowship complex, he often spent his out-of-school hours watching the planes and admiring their sleek lines. But at 19, another ambition began to grow in him. He attended a meeting in Sentani where a man spoke about God's rule and authority in each person's life. Usiel recognized these claims and committed himself to Christ. Out of this commitment came a desire to serve his people. This desire is now being realized as he translates God's Word for his own people.

Sonja Rehatta came from an old and highly-developed culture on the island of Java in Indonesia. The world of her physician father and English schoolteacher mother was a world surrounded by family, friends and the privileges of wealth and position. In this secure environment, Sonja lived her early girlhood happily unaware of the larger world about her.

In common with most Indonesians, Sonja believed in God. As she grew older, God's love took on greater meaning, inspiring her to leave her comfortable world and move to Irian Jaya. There Sonja took SIL's Cross-Cultural Communications Course (CCC) and learned how she could be involved in translation, linguistics and literacy work among Indonesian ethnic minorities.

During the course, Sonja and the other students studied the cultural differences and similarities they would face in this type of work. In one class, for instance, they discussed the different eating habits of people in various cultures. "The most common lament among Asian students

in America," said anthropology lecturer Marilyn Gregerson, "is having to eat all those mashed potatoes." The students, all of whom came from rice or sago-eating regions, readily empathized.

Jacob Bemey, another graduate of the CCC, cannot recall a time when he was not interested in translating the Word of God into Kemtuk, his mother tongue. In pursuit of this calling, he attended Bible school in Sentani. While there, he heard about a Dutchman named Jaap van der Wilden, who had just moved into a village near his home. The local gossip was that this man was trying to learn Kemtuk in order to translate God's Word into the Kemtuk language. Jacob quickly made Jaap's acquaintance and found the stories about Jaap to be true. With these shared goals, Jaap and Jacob became a team; together they translated the Gospels of John and Luke.

When the first CCC opened in 1980, Jaap saw the value of extra training for his enthusiastic co-translator and enrolled Jacob, never realizing just how valuable this training would be. Later, when family needs forced Jaap and his family to leave the Kemtuk project and return to the Netherlands, Jacob continued the translation, using the skills he had learned in the CCC course.

Today, men and women who speak Sentani and Kemtuk study the Scriptures translated by Usiel and Jacob. For long hours at a time, groups gather to hear Jacob and Usiel explain the "way of life" in the language they know best, and their needs are being met.

And Sonja? Her training continues, for her goal is to work with an unwritten language that she must first learn and analyze. Ultimately, like Usiel and Jacob, she hopes to take the Word to those who have yet to understand its message.

In 1973, on their first trip to the Beriks as a family, translator Peter Westrum (below), his wife Sue and 15 month-old David had to cross a large section of the South Pacific Ocean in an open 11-meter canoe. They then spent two long, hard, oppressively hot days on the Tor River. Today that journey is made in a 45-minute flight in a JAARS Helio Courier followed by a relatively safe half-hour of river travel.

Irian Jaya — Berik Literacy Project

The Berik people were excited the day Peter and Sue Westrum moved into the village of Tenwer. The path leading to the Westrums' new home was decorated with arched palm branches. Brandishing six-foot long wooden arrows that clattered against their bows, the Beriks smiled enthusiastically and welcomed the newcomers into their jungle village.

The journey up the tortuously winding Tor River had taken the Westrums two long days. During the entire trip their infant son, David, had been ill with a high fever and diarrhea. As the boat slipped past tall trees, undergrowth, river weeds, sago palms and thick jungle ferns, Sue, pregnant with her second child, prayed not only for the new life ahead, but for David's life. What a relief to arrive, to place the baby on a mattress inside their own house and to see the friendly faces of the Berik people!

While all this was new for Sue, it was not for Peter. He had been to Tenwer on two previous occasions. His initial visit had been with an Indonesian government official and fellow SIL colleagues, Norm Draper and Bob Sterner. On that first visit, Peter had been impressed with the neatness of this small jungle settlement and with the warm welcome he had received. One old lady, clinging to Peter's arm, had said haltingly in the national language, "You come back. Bring your wife and baby. Come help us." The invitation was accepted, the journey made, the arrival complete.

The job ahead, as Peter and Sue saw it, was to learn the language, compose a writing system, produce literature including Scripture, and teach

the people to read and write. They would also study the culture and help care for the Berik's medical needs.

For Berik speaker Esau Timbuat, the coming of the Westrums was especially significant. For years he had felt there was something more to life, something on the edge of his experience he had not yet touched. He knew there was a God out there, but did not know how He could be reached. Sensing the Westrums could help him with his quest, Esau accepted their invitation to help them learn his language. He also helped with the translation of a small book about Christ. Through this book in his language and other materials in the national language he, Esau Timbuat of the Tor River of Irian Jaya, discovered he could relate to God in a personal way and that God could relate to him.

Timbuat was also interested in reading. Educated through the sixth grade in Indonesian schools, he felt deeply the need for other Beriks to learn to read. In 1975, two years after the Westrums first began to live among the Berik people, Timbuat said, "While you're on furlough, I'm going to teach them myself!" But he could not. He had the will, but no method, no books, no tools to work with. He had to wait.

When the Westrums returned from furlough, the compilation of books became top priority. Timbuat, seeing that his people would need something to read after they had learned how, volunteered information for a book about everyday implements in Berik life. Later, he worked on two more books. One was a background aid to understanding Christ's life on earth, and the other, a health book that encouraged Beriks to keep flies off themselves and their food.

In the meantime, the Westrums created ways to motivate the Berik people to read. They put up notices and sent notes in Berik throughout the village. If villagers wanted Peter to get anything from town, he encouraged them to write down what they wanted. Eventually, the idea of reading and writing took hold. In an initial survey, 450 adults out of the total 1,000 Berik people registered their desire to learn to read and write.

Spurred on by this evidence of enthusiasm, the Westrums went to work. Their first task was to determine which sounds occurred most frequently in the Berik language. To do this, Sue took two or three pages of each style of writing and speaking they had collected and laboriously counted how many times each of the sounds was used.

After two weeks, Sue had a list that started with the most used sound and ended with the least used sound. Now she knew which sounds to teach first. She collected short, easy-to-read stories to include in each primer. In the end, with Timbuat's enthusiastic help, the Westrums published five primers ranging from pre-reading to the very advanced stages of literacy. Then they began trial literacy classes to see how well the people could learn to read with the new books. Timbuat watched in anticipation.

The Westrums' next-door neighbors, Dorsi and Matius, had observed the preparations for this new event for some time. Dorsi often wondered what exactly was going on. One day her curiosity overcame her shyness, and she asked what the evening activity meant.

"We're getting ready for reading classes," said Sue.

Up until that time, Dorsi's main responsibility

had been to look after her large family and garden. At night, after a long day spent tending her garden, she was too tired to think about learning to read.

The same was true for her husband, Matius. At the end of his day, he was content to relax on the raised porch of his thatched-roofed house and eat his supper of fish and sago.

Nevertheless, on the first day of classes, Dorsi showed up, baby on hip, and sat down for her first reading lesson. The experience was unlike any she had ever known. Instead of the harsh words and derision she had come to expect whenever she made an error, Dorsi was treated with kindness and encouragement.

As the days passed, Dorsi became exhilarated by this new experience. She was actually learning to read and write her own language. She discovered this was something she could do even with a nursing infant sprawled across her writing hand.

At first, Dorsi's husband, Matius, exhibited his lack of interest in the reading classes by staying home. However, Dorsi's excitement soon infected Matius, and he also joined the class. They were two of the 19 people who learned to read during that first literacy course.

In addition to learning to read their own language, two men also learned to read Bahasa Indonesian. Said one man, "A light went on in my head. I suddenly realized that each sound had a meaning, and if I said the sound for the symbol I could read."

Timbuat smiled with satisfaction. His dream was at last becoming a reality! The Berik people of the mighty Tor River were becoming literate. They would be able to read God's Word for themselves!

English Training In Indonesia

The ability to speak English is one of the most sought-after skills in the world today. Countries everywhere, seeking to compete on the open market, need to communicate in a common language. Most often that language is English. In addition, many high technology machines are imported from English-speaking countries, and their software is in English. As part of SIL's cooperative program with Cenderawasih University of Irian Jaya, SIL personnel are helping to teach English and other courses.

Eleanor Melville of Scotland is a teacher of English with the Indonesia Branch of the Summer Institute of Linguistics. She grew up in Kenya and Rhodesia, where she first developed an interest in other cultures. As an adult, she moved to England where she taught English to immigrants in East London and Birmingham. With an M.A. in Applied Linguistics, plus several years with a publishing company writing English language course materials and advising the publishers on the content of submitted articles, Eleanor is well prepared for her current assignment.

Eleanor and her colleagues, Letitia Saunders from the United States and Carol Sherk from Canada, have found that the nature of teaching and the students are different in Indonesia than they were in their homelands. But Letitia and Carol agree with Eleanor when she says, "I believe enthusiastically in the principle 'by love serve one another.' I know it's important for these university students to learn English. It is a great challenge for me to provide something they truly want and need."

T*he Philippines:* Seven thousand gem-like islands strung across a corner of the Pacific Ocean. Sparkling beaches, pine-scented forests, fertile valleys — the variety of terrain staggers the imagination.

Ifugao Province: In northern Luzon, crown jewel of the chain. Fairyland of emerald mountains. Verdant cloisonne of rice terraces.

The Ifugao people: Handsome. Proud. Diligent. Descendants of men and women who 200 years before Christ's birth rearranged their razor-sharp mountains into an elaborate series of rock-bound rice terraces.

The striking folk arts of the Philippines counterpoint the intense landscapes of the islands. From the Yakan weavings of the south to the fantastic rice terraces of the north, color is the hallmark of the country.

But it is the faces of the people that arrest the attention of any visitor. Products of an ancient melting pot, Filipinos are not only handsome, but open and eager to learn.

Philippines —
Paradise Lost, Paradise Found

Long before the West discovered her, the Philippines traded with India, Siam, Sumatra, China and Japan. Sanskrit words joined the language. Chinese and Japanese business methods, utensils and tools became part of Filipino life.

Then in 1521 the Spaniard Ferdinand Magellan discovered the Philippines. That was the beginning of 300 years of Spanish rule. Their influence, too, was indelible.

At the turn of this century, the United States took control. English joined Spanish and Tagalog as a national language. Roads and railways were constructed and trade increased.

With the end of World War II came the independence of the Philippines. The nation began to create its own destiny. Believing themselves to be children of Malakas and Maganda — the Adam and Eve of folklore — the Filipinos invested their inherent strength and beauty in creating a nation that is deeply and uniquely their own.

Through all the political changes, the Ifugao people, descendants of the first Malay invasion, remained isolated. Literally carving a life out of the mountains, they remained untouched by the outside world. Their homes, clothing and art all exhibited a striking functional beauty that reflected their surroundings.

At the end of the war, a few outsiders began to trek into the remote Ifugao area. At least two archeologists paid for their uninvited arrival with their lives: they were beheaded.

But by 1953, when Len and Doreen Newell hiked in, the Ifugao were more accustomed to seeing strangers, though still suspicious. The Newells had come to bring God's Word to the

Ifugao, despite warnings in Manila that "those people cannot be converted!"

Len recalls, "It was an arduous trip. Ifugao is one of the most rugged sections of all southeast Asia. Often the trail is less than a foot wide, sometimes with only toeholds. The mountains are vertical. We discovered that the women can plant their gardens without bending over. It is not un-

usual for someone to fall out of her garden to her death. It is no wonder that the Ifugao could remain isolated for centuries."

The area is a natural paradise. The fantastic rice terraces add to the beauty of the rugged mountains. Wooden shovels, stone-tipped crowbars and human muscle created this "eighth wonder of the world" over 2,000 years ago. It has been

estimated that, end-to-end, the terraces would equal ten Great Walls of China, or reach halfway around the world.

The Ifugao are animists. Their lives are controlled by their attempts to appease approximately 1,200 spirits. Their religion, one of the most complex systems in all of Asia, is intricately related to everyday life. Anything that occurs without a reasonable explanation is credited to the spirits. "The spirit is trying to get our attention," the Ifugao explain.

The Ifugao believe that the spirits must enter humans in order to express their desires. When this happens, great negotiating takes place. The spirit makes his demands, and gifts and sacrifices must be made to pacify his anger.

Remembering an occasion during his early days with the Ifugao, Len says, "A baby was quite ill. I was called to the house, but was not asked to assist. For several days, the medium made exorbitant demands on the already poor family. Many pigs and chickens were sacrificed. A great deal of rice wine and other gifts were offered. But in the end, the tiny girl died.

"The night after the child was buried, someone noticed that her grandfather was missing. Finally, they noticed a flickering light on the hillside near the grave site. When some of the family reached the spot, the old man was threatening to kill himself.

From the north to the south, Filipinos are still partial to their traditional bright clothing. Nearly isolated from the outside world until World War II, the Ifugaos have managed a remarkable

blend of the old ways and the new. They utilize everything from modern watches to the routine bolo knife.

At first, the Ifugaos were unsure about accepting the Gospel. But hearing it, and

then seeing it, in their own language opened their hearts to the message of God's love. Copies of the Ifugao New Testament quickly show the signs of frequent use (below).

"Moaning again and again that life was hopeless, he cried out at the injustice of the Ifugao spirits. No matter how hard the people tried, they could never satisfy the spirits.

"I saw once again, in that agonizing moment, the tremendous need for the Ifugao to have God's Word in their own language. That seeming paradise in the mountains was in fact a hell of fear and hopelessness!"

The Newells continued in their language study and translation work. As often happens with translators, Len saw the first Ifugaos accept Christ as Savior at the translation desk. They felt the Holy

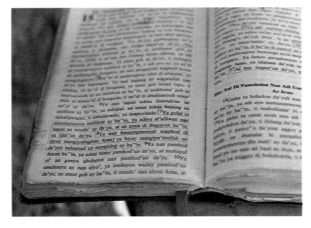

Spirit speak to them through the actual translation process.

Said one translation helper, "My father taught me how to perform the rituals of a *mumba'i* (spirit priest). I enjoyed the rice wine and receiving meat for my reward. I believed I was an important man in our place because all the people trusted me as the *mumba'i*.

"When we translated Acts 13:6-12, I found out about Paul's encounter with Elymas, the sorcerer who went blind. That night I kept wondering if I would go blind like that *mumba'i*. I began to study what we had translated during the day.

"We continued translating, and I discovered Acts 19:19 where they burned the books of sacrificing. Right then I decided that I was a sinner. I accepted the Lord Jesus into my heart. Now I am working to serve Him. My family and I are very happy because I turned away from drinking, sacrificing and all the bad things I had been doing."

By January, 1972, there were nine Christians in the village of Batad where the Newells lived. A Balangao believer named Ama came from across the mountains to baptize the new believers.

Then in early June, just before the Newells were to leave for furlough, seven Ifugao men from a village across a range of mountains walked into Batad. They had heard about Jesus Christ when a Batad Ifugao had visited their home. They wanted to know more about how to become Christians.

Before the seven men reached the Newells' house, the spirit priests of Batad intercepted them. For almost two days, the priests virtually held the men prisoners trying to convince them that Christianity was wrong for the Ifugao. Discouraged, five of the men finally returned home.

Acquiring a workable vo-cabulary and an under-standing of the grammar structure required a tre-mendous amount of trans-lator Len Newell's time. Of-ten, it came in the unex-

pected — and sometimes hard to accept — blessing of interruptions from the villa-gers seeking help or conver-sation (right).

But in the process, signifi-cant relationships were de-

veloped with the people. Trust and affection were es-tablished which later helped the Ifugaos accept the Scrip-tures (below).

The remaining two managed to get to the Newells' house and declare their interest. Runners were sent to gather all the Christians. A time of testimony, prayer and song led to the conversion of the two visitors. Then the Batad elders returned with the new believers to their village.

Before Len left for Canada on furlough, he made the long trek to Padyay where the two men lived. He was astounded to find dozens of Christians. Sharing their newfound faith had come as second nature to the two men, and their neighbors had joined them in their belief in Jesus Christ. The Newells left for their furlough thrilled with the power of God's Word and the leading of the Holy Spirit among the Ifugao.

Five years passed before Len Newell returned to the Philippines. His wife, Doreen, had contracted leukemia and in 1975 went to be with the Lord.

In April, 1977, Len and his new bride, Jo, hiked into Ifugao. Over a period of three weeks, they visited 12 of the 32 churches that had sprung up since 1972. To their amazement, they found over 3,000 believers! There had been no missionaries, no trained pastors and no evangelists in the area. The Christians had simply relied on the Holy Spirit to "shepherd" them.

The Ifugao used a method of sharing God's Word that fit their culture perfectly — argumentation. Although many Westerners are un-

comfortable with arguments, the contest of logic clearly communicates the Word of God to the hearts of the Ifugao.

In the early days of the Ifugao church, Len was alarmed to discover many Christians passing over references to God's love in favor of passages dealing with God's judgment. One verse that spoke to the people in those days was Matthew 10:28: "Do not be afraid of those who kill the body but cannot kill the soul. Rather, be afraid of the one who can destroy both soul and body in hell" (NIV).

When Len questioned the elders about this emphasis, they answered, "From antiquity, we have paid attention to those spirits which could

do us the most harm, who could inflict the most judgment. We didn't need to pay attention to a spirit that would do us no harm."

Then Len understood. Nevertheless, he was pleased that, as the Christians grew in their faith, they began to understand and appreciate the love of God.

In April, 1982, the first Ifugao Bible Conference was held. Over 1,000 people came to Batad from all across Ifugao. The theme was "Praises to God our Heavenly Father." Sessions ran from one to four hours, with preaching, Bible study, testimonies, and music. On Palm Sunday, the group gathered in one of the rice terrace streams for the baptism of 40 new believers.

The Newells' prayers have been answered beyond their fondest dreams. Instead of one church, there are over 80; instead of a few believers, there are thousands, and their numbers continue to grow.

To assist the newly formed Ifugao church,

John 1:1 in Ifugao

Hidin hopapnah agguy ni' nalmuwan an amin di logom, ya wagwada tuwalih Kristu, an ma'alih Punhapiton Apo Dios. Ya nihihinnah Apo Dios, ya hiyah Apo Dios tuwali.

In the beginning was the Word, and the Word was with God, and the Word was God.

Christian workers from other organizations are developing literacy programs and Bible training programs for church leaders.

The literacy program is a specific answer to the Ifugao prayers. The Scriptures in their own language have been an obvious blessing to them, but since only three percent are able to read, the Word of God is basically inaccessible to the other 97 percent. Most villages have two to four readers; some churches have no readers. As one woman put it, "It is no wonder we get defeated in our spiritual lives and cannot cope with the powers of darkness. We cannot read so we cannot go to the Word of God and get the answers and be fed."

85

Ifugao hymns aid in meaningful worship services (left). But the first Ifugao believers have not been satisfied to keep the Gospel to themselves. From the beginning, they have felt the Lord leading them into evangelistic work (right). Carrying their supplies on their backs and Bible study materials in their shoulder bags, the evangelists crisscross the terraces and mountains of the Ifugao area giving the Lord's message to whoever will listen.

so they decided to do something
   about it.
They said they would learn
   to speak our language.
so they could write what was said
   in that Book
   in our language
so we could know what it said.

That Book is a miracle to us
   because it tells us
      Whom we should worship
      and that His name is God.

It also tells us why He did it.
   It is because He loves us very much.
If we follow His ways
   we will live with Him forever.

When we read that Book,
   it is God talking to us.
He is talking to us Ifugao people.

This Book that is made
   is written in our Ifugao language,
   and we have accepted
      what is written
      in that Book.

That is why we are gathered today
   and rejoice —
because we have with us
   the Book of Life.

There is no doubt about the value the Ifugao place on the Word of God. When the Ifugao New Testament was dedicated, one leader read a poem:

   . . . There were some people who came
      from a faraway land.
   They looked different;
      their ways were different;
      and they spoke a different language.

   They had with them a Book.
   But we did not know what was written
      in that Book,

The miracle of the Book of Life has spread throughout Ifugao. That fairyland filled with fear, that paradise lost, has become Paradise Found for thousands of Ifugaos as they have placed their trust in God.

AFRICA

Africa. The very name calls to mind a multitude of images. More than 50 nations share its land, many with names unfamiliar to those who studied world geography more than ten years ago.

The continent displays incredible contrasts in topography and climate — barren deserts, scorching hot by day and cold by night; luxuriant rain forests, warm and humid; vast stretches of rolling grasslands, home to great herds of antelope, gazelle and wildebeest.

Its people also illustrate the contrast which is Africa. From the Arabic culture of the north to the great tribal kingdoms south of the Sahara, Africa reflects the cultural and linguistic treasures of its peoples — speakers of some 1,600 languages.

Over 500 African languages now have at least a part of the Bible. SIL is currently working in more than 150 languages while other groups work in an additional 200 language groups. Yet much work remains to be done.

An increasing number of Africans are joining in the translation task. National Bible organizations have been established in Nigeria, Ghana, Kenya and other African nations. Dedicated African Christians like Justin Frempong of Ghana and Jean Pierre of Cameroon, described in the following chapters, are assuming an ever-increasing responsibility in the work of Bible translation.

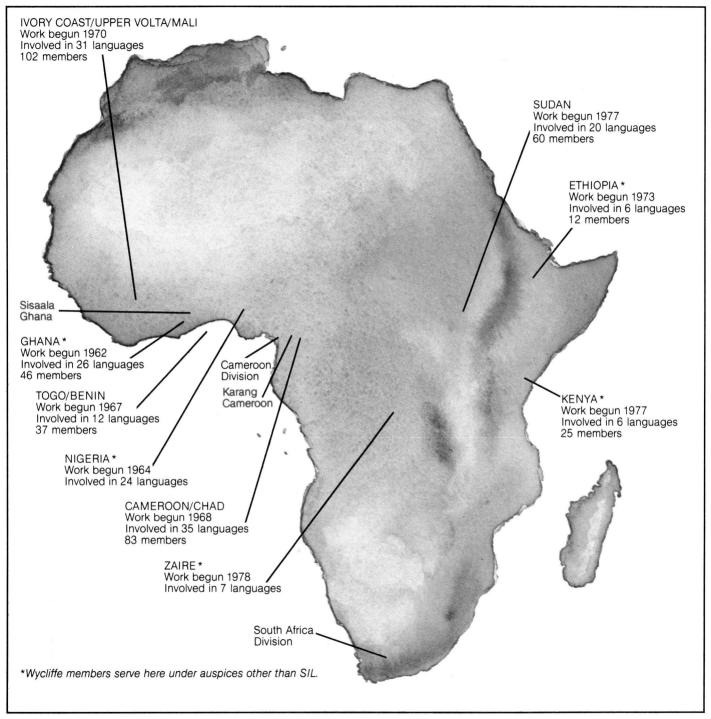

IVORY COAST/UPPER VOLTA/MALI
Work begun 1970
Involved in 31 languages
102 members

SUDAN
Work begun 1977
Involved in 20 languages
60 members

ETHIOPIA *
Work begun 1973
Involved in 6 languages
12 members

Sisaala
Ghana

GHANA *
Work begun 1962
Involved in 26 languages
46 members

Cameroon
Division

Karang
Cameroon

KENYA *
Work begun 1977
Involved in 6 languages
25 members

TOGO/BENIN
Work begun 1967
Involved in 12 languages
37 members

NIGERIA *
Work begun 1964
Involved in 24 languages

CAMEROON/CHAD
Work begun 1968
Involved in 35 languages
83 members

ZAIRE *
Work begun 1978
Involved in 7 languages

South Africa
Division

*Wycliffe members serve here under auspices other than SIL.

Cameroon — Partnership in Translation

Cameroon has been called "Africa in miniature" with its tropical forests, dusty savannah, and rapidly developing cities and villages rich in traditional culture. There is linguistic variety, too. The official languages are French and English, but over 200 different tribal languages are also spoken.

Although Bible translation has been done in several major language groups, the majority of the ethnic minorities do not have the Scriptures in their mother tongue. While the United Bible Societies and other missions are working in some languages, a vast task remains, one that demands dedication and careful strategy. How can God's Word be made available in so many different languages?

The Summer Institute of Linguistics uses several strategies in Cameroon. In all of them SIL cooperates closely with the Cameroon people.

In some language groups, the SIL team lives among the people and learns their language. The translation process is a partnership: the SIL team knows the meaning of the Scripture to be translated, and the Cameroonian knows the best way to express that meaning in his own language. As they say in Cameroon: "It takes more than one hand to tie a bundle."

In other language groups there is no SIL team, and the translation project is under the direction of a local speaker—a Christian who longs to see God's Word in his own language. Frequently such translators come from groups where a church already exists, but where it is still relying on Scriptures in some other language. SIL people train these Cameroonians in principles of translation and offer regular help with biblical exegesis.

Wearing traditional dress, a Karang chief (far left) holds a ceremonial sword. Karang leaders feel the responsibility of guiding Karang people into the modern world while still retaining cultural identity.

The setting sun casts long shadows as weary Karang, the day's work done, head home to the village (left).
(Below) A mask worn by boys during puberty rites at which they are initiated into manhood.

91

The Karang of Cameroon

The rainy season was just beginning that day in 1978 when Ed and Ginny Ubels first drove into the Karang village. The drive to the village was slow and slippery. When they arrived, they were given a grass-roofed house that leaked in a dozen places. But when they saw the transformation the rain brought the countryside, they quickly forgot their inconveniences. The parched dry savannah was turned into lush green farmland.

Ed and Ginny soon learned that the cool evening hours were best for language learning. With their day's work complete, the Karang were free to chat; they liked to discuss their culture with the Ubels. One thing Ginny learned about was the variety of ingredients used in the Karangs' tasty meals. No processed foods here; nothing from the supermarket — everything was home-grown. Their specialties were corn, rice, millet, peanuts, sesame and more than 100 different kinds of green vegetables.

Ed enjoyed the Karang folktales he heard around the campfires at night. But whatever the evening's topic, the conversation usually returned to the subject of farming — who was planting what, when and where. The younger generation talked of little but cotton, the crop that "turned into money."

Ed and Ginny learned that a national company was helping the Karang by linking them with the national economy. The company surfaced the roads and built bridges. It provided cottonseed, fertilizer, insecticide, oxen, ploughs, tractors, agricultural training and factories to gin cotton. It also introduced new food crops and crop rotation.

The Ubels noticed that peddlers followed close

Ed Ubels (far left), a translator from Michigan, quickly learned that the cool evening hours were best for language learning. Sooner or later the conversation always turned to farming — the Karang's livelihood.

The Karang are a loving and family oriented people. In a quiet moment, a Karang father holds his child in his lap (left).

Excellent farmers (bottom), the Karang grow a wide variety of grains and more than a hundred different kinds of green vegetables.

behind the cotton markets. It was easy to entice the women into buying enamel dishes to replace their calabash bowls. And what woman could resist a fine bright cotton wrap-around and head scarf, not to mention earrings and beads! The men bought beautiful long robes or western-style leisure suits, bicycles, radios, watches and lanterns, as well as cement and tin to replace thatched-roof and mud houses. It was a time of rapid change, a time when traditional ways were meeting new ways.

Of course, not everyone welcomed the new ways. The elderly Karangs were much like the older generation anywhere. Karang grandpas sighed and said that boys and girls used to be more mature in the days when they endured long months of training in initiation camps. There they learned respect, self-discipline, obedience and strength. Grandpas spoke of the courage it took to defend their families with spears and boomerangs against neighboring wife-raiding clans. They reflected on days of leisure, traveling from village to village, visiting their friends and sharing bowl after bowl of home-brewed millet beer. They sang about the glory of the hunt, the success of the fishing expedition and the health of the family. They recalled the displeasure of dead ancestors when the clan did not interact harmoniously and the inevitable harm that befell those in the path of the angry spirits. Some young people listened and reflected on their grandpa's words. Many others listened with deaf ears, their thoughts on today, not their grandpa's time.

Ed and Ginny saw it as a special time. It was a time to reflect on one's relationship with the eternal, true God and on one's place in a changing world; a time when people were ready for

God's Word to penetrate their lives.

The Karangs had heard the Good News of Jesus Christ in the 1960's when some teenage boys heard the Gospel at a boarding school and took the message home to their families. Soon after that, missionaries came to work among the people, and whole villages became Christian. They built chapels and sent away some of their choice young men to Bible school. Later, these young men became leaders of the church. Their ministry was hampered, however, by the fact that they had to preach, teach and pray in the trade language. They longed to work in their own language and were delighted when SIL responded to their request for help by sending the Ubels.

One of Ed Ubels's many Karang friends was David. Ed and David spent hours at night talking about such things as where the earth and sky meet, why the annual rains hadn't started yet, and why Abraham did wrong in fathering a child by Hagar when Sarah was barren. Like Abraham, David also had a barren wife and had fathered a child by a second wife. He knew what it was to have a bitter wife and a jealous wife, wives who refused to share household chores and threatened each other with spells and potions. He was searching for God's peace.

Could God speak to David or to his wife in their own language? Once this idea seemed impossible to most Karangs. They were convinced that no one of importance ever spoke Karang. They never heard or read anything in Karang at a government office, the school, the medical dispensary or the church.

The Ubels found themselves battling this attitude. Much of their energy in the early days went into village visits where their conversation

No "Freezing" Please

Ginney Ubels had always had a hard time picking up a new language. When she and her husband Ed went to northern Cameroon to learn the trade language, she frequently was unable to understand what was being said to her. Then she would freeze, becoming totally unable to respond. It took several months for her to feel at ease in the language-learning situation.

When Ed and Ginny were ready to move into the Karang language, both of them had that scary feeling that comes from facing a new language-learning situation, and this time the language was unwritten. Ginny prayed that the Lord would somehow keep her from going through the long "freezing" process again.

During the first few days in the village Ginny went to the village well daily to get their water. She had learned how to greet the Karang women there and to say, "I've come to get water," and "I'm going home now." She practiced these three phrases on everyone she met, and all the ladies responded in kind.

A few weeks later Ginny and Ed went to the nearest town to do some shopping and to meet the local government leader. His first words to Ginny were, "So you're the lady who is learning to speak the Karang language so fast."

The word had really spread! The Karang people were impressed by the enormous attempts she was making to learn their language. Somehow her efforts touched them and made them open to her gestures of friendship. The people build up her language learning successes; and since she began to learn Karang, she has never had that freezing experience!

went something like this:

"Who gave you and your forefathers your language?"

"God did."

"What language do you use when your hearts are heavy, when you cry out in sorrow? What language do you use when you are happy, when you sing at work in your fields? Isn't it Karang? Is the God who gave you your language unable to understand you? Of course He understands. He wants to talk with you. He wants to hear you cry out to Him the sorrows of your heart. He wants to hear your songs of joy in the language He gave you."

"But how can we sing? There is no songbook in Karang. How can we pray? There is no Christian teaching in Karang."

"When you sing in the fields, are you holding a book in one hand and a hoe with the other? When you sit beside your lost one, do you read a book to mourn your sorrow? No, you simply express what you feel. Please don't be ashamed of it. Even though your language is not yet written, speak with God, pray and sing. Begin now and someday we will help you write those songs and put them together in a hymnal. We'll help you learn more about the God to whom you speak and who speaks to you through His written Word."

In 1980, before Ed and Ginny left on furlough, they wrote down the songs that had been composed during the previous year. They mimeographed 500 copies of a ten-page songsheet and gave them to the church leaders to sell. When they returned a year later, not one hymnal was left. They printed 250 more and that edition sold out in two weeks. There was no Karang primer and no Karang reading classes, yet 750 songsheets were sold.

After clearing a field for planting, everyone celebrates. Home-made beer, made from a fermented mixture of flour and millet, is served in calibash bowls.

The evening fire is a time to learn the history and folk legends of the Karang. David (right), is one of many who spent hours with Ed, teaching him Karang and later, talking about the deep questions of life.

Working in the fields (far right) with friends, Ed learned a lot about Karang culture and needs. A national company recently introduced cotton as a cash crop and brought rapid changes to the Karang way of life.

Today new Karang songs reach the Ubels from far and wide. A second collection has been printed and a third is being readied for printing.

The popularity of the songsheets was not the only encouraging news that awaited Ed and Ginny when they returned from their furlough. When they left, they were unsure whether or not the Karangs were interested in assuming any responsibility for the Karang translation and literacy project. When they returned, they found a literature committee functioning. It had already raised money to help pay for a mimeograph machine. Today there is a network of local committees tied together by a central committee, and the Karangs are actively involved in the entire program.

Before their furlough, Ed and Ginny did not have a regular language assistant. Soon after they returned, Jean Pierre Yapele offered to work with them and has since become a skilled co-worker. Together they have translated several New Testament books and prepared materials for a literacy program.

Translation work began in Karang because the people asked for it. Now, because of their active participation, their dream of Scriptures in Karang, understood and read by Karangs, is rapidly becoming a reality.

A Couple for All Reasons

Living and working in a new culture can be emotionally exhausting, as Ed and Ginny learned. "It's not being a linguist or a Bible translator that is exhausting," say the Ubels. "Rather, it's determining with the Karang what our role among them should be. Many of them feel we should supply things like money, clothes, coffee, soap, envelopes and paper. Others look for services such as:

— typing service
— taxi service
— towing service
— ambulance driver
— medicine dispenser
— employer
— English teacher
— foster parent
— preacher
— seamstress
— driver's training instructor
— carpenter
— cassette, radio, watch and bicycle repairman
— buyer of goods available only in the big cities.

"Every 'yes' means time lost from language work and increased demands. Every 'no' means a feeling of having refused a cup of cold water. A 'yes' may mean a three-day trip to the hospital, a saved life, and three more ambulance requests the next week. A 'no' may mean a dead mother. We are learning to pray every day about our yes's and no's. We are trying to work out how putting the Word on the printed page relates to living it."

Cameroon Translation Workshop

Children are welcome at the women's literacy classes taught by Ginny Ubels in the local church building (far left). Karang is a tonal language. Though most words are one syllable in length, the pitch the word is given can alter its meaning.

Books in hand, more and more women attend classes as enthusiasm for reading increases (left).

Paul Djafki (below, at left) and Jean-Pierre (at right) attend a workshop for national translators. After translating the last three chapters of Luke, Paul Djafki visited several churches at Easter time and preached from the text. Many people expressed their deep appreciation for the Scriptures in their own language.

Translation workshops are held three times a year," says Mona Perrin, head of SIL's translation department in Cameroon. "The purpose of these SIL-staffed seminars is to help the mother-tongue translators tackle the New Testament book by book."

A typical workshop day begins with an informal time of worship and prayer. Sharing is relaxed, and the fellowship stimulating. Then the hard work begins as the translators and instructors discuss the Scripture passage of the day. There is good rapport between the staff and translators, and everyone enjoys the sessions.

"We have two important points to cover in each passage," continues Mona. "Everyone needs to understand exactly what the passage means. That's exegesis. Then we need to discuss ways of clearly expressing the meaning in each language. That's translation. We also discuss potential translation problems."

After these discussion periods, each man goes away to translate the passage by himself. He works from an exegetical "display" based on the Greek text and prepared by SIL members. This analysis of the passage, simply arranged, clearly shows the way each thought relates to the next. The men work from several French or English translations as well. They translate ten or twelve verses every day until the book is finished.

Later, the men write what each translated word means in French or English. This is called back-translation and enables the staff to check the translation with the mother-tongue translator. Out of this teamwork emerges a good quality translation.

During the evening the men relax together, tell

stories and sometimes play games. Occasionally, sessions are held to discuss the use of Scripture and ways to help people learn to read. Some languages have not been written long, and the translators want to encourage literacy among their own people.

Many of the trainees see for the first time what Scriptures in their mother tongue can mean. They become enthusiastic and determined to translate. One trainee, a university graduate named Joseph Mfonyam, is now an SIL member. He and his wife, Rebecca, expect to work on the translation into Bafut, Joseph's own language.

Since 1977, men from about 70 languages have received basic training at the annual courses in Cameroon. French speakers now train in Yaounde while English speakers train in Bamenda, the center of English-speaking Cameroon.

Some Cameroonian mother-tongue translators have realized the need to train local people to check the translators' work and have organized reviewers courses in different parts of Cameroon. SIL consultants have provided the training.

"I've been privileged," says Mona, joy sparkling in her eyes, "as I've been allowed to cross cultural barriers and get to know these people. We have

such different backgrounds, yet we've enjoyed deep fellowship together and grown to appreciate each other more and more. I've learned much from their walk with the Lord while they've learned about the Scriptures and the technical aspects of translation from us. It really is a two-way fellowship!"

Jean Pierre Yapele

Jean Pierre Yapele was in high school when the civil war in Chad broke out. This tragic event closed down his school, and he returned to his home in Cameroon to help his father farm their land.

Jean Pierre's only book was a French Bible — a book he read repeatedly. On Sundays, as he read the church liturgy, he would wonder whether he should be in seminary. When he finally decided to apply, he was placed on a two-year waiting list.

In the meantime, Jean Pierre heard about the Karang literature committee. The committee was looking for a young Karang speaker with enough formal education to help in a literacy program, and Jean Pierre wondered if he could qualify. A few weeks later the committee sent SIL workers Ed and Ginny Ubels to Jean Pierre's village.

Said Jean Pierre, "In just two weeks, Ed and Ginny taught me to read and write in my language. I wouldn't have believed it possible!"

Unlike most workshop participants, Jean Pierre is not a pastor or a teacher. He has never been to Bible school or seminary. Nor is he old enough, according to African culture, to have earned respect as a leader in his community. Nevertheless he does have a crucial role in the Karang translation program. He is a semi-independent translator — the indispensable counterpart to the SIL team.

Although he still needs Ed and Ginny to help him understand the meaning of the biblical text, he has the ability to express that meaning in clear, natural Karang — a skill that might take the Ubels a decade or more to develop.

He is also skilled at thinking through how his own people will perceive the message of the translated Scriptures. During one workshop, he and other participants were studying Revelation 5:8, which says that 24 elders bowed down to worship the Lamb. He thought of his own people bowing, head touching the ground, before their earthly ruler, and asked a very pertinent question: "Did they want to or were they forced to?" His question may have prevented a translation that somehow transformed the elders' joyful expression of adoration into a forced act of obedience.

The Ubels say, "Jean Pierre is our co-translator, co-editor, co-everything. Besides his skill as a translator, he is also a writer, typist, editor and literacy teacher. He is growing in his understanding of God's Word and its implications for him personally and for the Karang in their cultural situation.

"Jean Pierre has also observed what learning to read can do for a person's self-image and has seen how powerfully the translated text communicates. All this has increased his commitment to Bible translation and to serving his own people."

Leonard Bolioki

When Leonard Bolioki first attended a translation principles course, he was a church member, but his life was largely unaffected by his religion. During the course he was impressed by the prayer life of others; people were really talking to God! Every time he opened the Bible he was challenged. He later attended other translation workshops and translated the Scriptures into Yambetta at his home.

After Leonard finished translating Mark's Gospel, he discovered some Bible study notes on Mark's Gospel and took them back to his village. These he used daily in his family prayer time. As he read the passage from his translation and asked questions from the Bible study notes, he and his family were enriched. He is now a committed Christian, following the Lord.

Paul Djafki

Paul Djafki comes from a remote mountainous region in northern Cameroon. "Even though we Matal people are tucked away in the mountains," says Paul, "God has not forgotten us. He loves us and has sent His Word — even to us."

When Paul returned home from an SIL workshop with the translated Easter story, he read it to a group of his friends. To his great joy, seven people committed their lives to the Lord.

Seriously committed to Bible translation, Paul

has developed his own work pattern. Mornings are spent translating the biblical text; afternoons are used for revising and typing the morning's work. Then in the cool of the evening, Paul sits on his doorstep and leads an informal prayer meeting and Bible study. This allows him to test the translated Scriptures for clarity and naturalness as he reads the Scriptures to first-time hearers. If Paul is unable to be present at his evening meeting, he records the newly-translated passage for that day on his cassette recorder. Later, when the people gather for what has become an important community event, Paul's wife plays the pre-recorded tape.

When Paul is questioned about the high incidence of people turning to the Lord and the rapid growth of the church, he replies without hesitation, "It is because of the daily reading of Scripture."

Andrew Doucha

Because Andrew Doucha spoke no English and very little French when he came to the first translation workshop in 1977, he brought a schoolboy with him to interpret. After the course, he was determined to learn French, and bought a French Bible. When he is asked how

John Watters, an SIL member working in the Ejagham language, often visited an elderly neighbor who was suffering from leprosy. Whenever he tried to talk to his neighbor about the Lord, the old man laughed. One day when John passed by with a booklet of passages from Mark's Gospel, he stopped to greet the old man.

"What do you have in your hand," asked the man.

"It's part of God's Word in your language. But you won't be interested in that."

"Come on, show me what it is."

"No, it's God's Word. I'm just taking it to the Christian meeting. It's not for you. You wouldn't be interested."

His curiosity piqued, the old man demanded John read him what was in the book.

John read the passage from Mark where the leper came to Jesus. When he finished, he asked the man if he understood. But the man was too moved to speak.

The next day there was a knock at John's door. It was the old man, and he had brought the chief with him.

"I've come because I want you to read that book to us," he said. "Please go and get it so the chief can hear it, too."

"I don't know if our neighbor ever came to know the Lord before he died," John said. "But he made me realize that many may seem to reject the message at first only because they have never understood what it is about. Deep down many people are waiting to hear the Good News, but they need to hear it in a language they understand."

he learned French so quickly, he says, "I can't explain it. The Lord just gave it to me."

Andrew has attended all the translation workshops. These have enabled him to translate nearly all of the New Testament in six years. The books that yet remain to be translated are John, Acts, II Corinthians and II Timothy. The workshops have also taught him the importance of testing his first-draft translated passages in his home area.

Andrew tells about a neighbor who was saved through the newly-translated Scriptures.

"This man and his family never came to church, but I began to befriend him and read some Bible passages to him. Finally he came to know the Lord. He bought all the books available in the language and would come to my house with Peter's epistles, open the pages and say, 'The Lord will show us the passage, then I want you to read it to me.' I would read the passage, and he would leave satisfied. A few days later he would return and tell me from memory almost all that was in the passage we had read. His wife and family, however, continued to resist the Gospel.

"One day the man fell sick with an extremely high fever. I stayed and prayed with him all night, but the Lord did not grant healing, and he was taken to the hospital. I continued to visit and pray with him, but the Lord chose to take him and he died. His family appreciated my care for him and allowed me to go on visiting them. Eventually all the family became believers. Later, they found all my friend's books wrapped up among his possessions, and they learned to read.

"I was deeply touched that the Lord loved my friend so much He called him into fellowship with Himself and then gave him six months to walk with Him on earth before taking him home."

Sharing the Vision

A Ghanaian man was asked to start a meeting in prayer. He stood hesitantly and started to pray in Twi, the most commonly spoken Ghanaian language. "God in heaven," he said, "we thank You for all the things You have made. But You know I do not speak Twi well. And I know that You do not speak my language. So I am finished. Amen."

Incidents like this continue to motivate a group of dedicated Christians, both Ghanaian and non-Ghanaian, to demonstrate that God does speak all the languages of Ghana.

The beginnings of SIL involvement in this country go back to 1958 when John Agamah, now a ranking Ghanaian police officer, was a student in England. He came in contact with members of SIL who asked him to serve as a language helper in their training course, giving students exposure to an African language. After this experience, John went to SIL administrators and made an impassioned plea for the Bibleless peoples of Ghana. In 1962 SIL began fieldwork in Ghana.

Since then, John and other Ghanaians, along with SIL personnel, have worked toward involving Ghanaian Christians fully in the work of Bible translation. In 1971 the Ghana Institute of Linguistics (GIL) was incorporated to help accomplish this goal. In 1980 SIL transferred its assets and activities to GIL, which was renamed the Ghana Institute of Linguistics, Literacy and Bible Translation (GILLBT). John Agamah and other Ghanaians serve as trustees and members of the executive committee.

Perhaps the spirit of GILLBT is best illustrated by the story of what happened among the Sisaala people of northern Ghana.

Life Changing Incidents in Ghana

Alendu Marifa: The First Sisaala Christian

Good-natured laughter rang out in the mud-walled courtyard. Alendu looked up. What was going on? Ah yes, the SIL women, Margrit Haudenschild and Gertrud Sopp, were visiting again.

"What did I say wrong?" one asked in faltering Sisaala.

Chuckling, one of the Sisaala women explained that by using the wrong tone on a word, Margrit had said something very different from what she meant to say.

"Thank you," Margrit said, and carefully practiced the proper tone on that troublesome word.

Finishing their conversation with the women, Margrit and Gertrud approached Alendu and began the long string of greetings appropriate to the Sisaala culture:

"Good morning, Alendu."
"Good morning."
"How are you?"
"I am well."
"How did you sleep?"
"I slept well."
"Have the mosquitos left you?"
"Yes, they have left me."
"Has the cold of the night left you?"
"Yes, it has left me."
"How is your father?"
"He is well."
"How is your mother?"
"She is well."

Yes, Alendu thought as he continued chatting with Margrit and Gertrud, these women really are learning to speak our language. They are learning

Sisaala woman goes to the village well for water (left), which is precious in hot, dry northern Ghana.

Alendu Marifa (right) was typical of the Sisaala people who befriended the SIL team. He encouraged their

language learning efforts and helped them understand his culture. He also listened to their testimony of Christ and decided he wanted this for himself. "I gave everything I had to Christ," he says.

to act like Sisaalas, too. That's good.

Alendu and the other Sisaalas in the village of Nabugabele were proud of their heritage. They told the SIL women traditional stories and explained their beliefs, their respect for their ancestors and their fear of evil spirits. They also introduced them to local foods — yams, antelope, and the thick, slightly sour grain porridge which they ate with dried fish and leaf sauces.

When Margrit and Gertrud first moved into town, Alendu did not understand why they were there. Then he heard that, like Ron and Mu Rowland before them, they'd come to translate the Book about Jesus Christ into Sisaala. Alendu had heard about Christ from Ron, and he had been intrigued.

One evening Alendu went to see the women and listened to them tell stories from the Bible. That night he dreamed that he was a Christian and was teaching others about Christ.

The next morning, after thinking about his dream, Alendu committed his life to Christ, becoming the very first Sisaala believer. Before long others became believers as well, and on Sundays nearly a dozen people gathered for worship.

Hungry to learn more, Alendu spent almost every evening with Margrit and Gertrud, soaking up all they could tell him about Christ. Soon he wanted to share his new-found joy and went to tell the Good News to people in Kurobele, 9 miles away. Many of these people responded to the message. Anxious to learn more, they began walking or cycling to Alendu's village for Sunday services.

Then, the rainy season came, making it difficult for the Kurobele people to come for meetings, and Alendu and Margrit decided to start meet-ings in Kurobele. Often they walked there together, enjoying three hours of fellowship on the way. Other times, Margrit went alone on her bicycle.

Between Kurobele and the village where Margrit and Alendu lived lay the village of Nmanduong. Margrit's frequent trips through town raised the curiosity of the people who lived there, and they finally asked Margrit to stop and tell them what she was doing. God used their curiosity to draw them to Himself.

Lutie Abudu: Faithful Teacher in Nmanduong

Sitting under a huge mango tree, the people of Nmanduong listened attentively to Margrit as she told them about Jesus Christ and her desire to translate His message into Sisaala. Even after she had finished, they sat quietly, contemplating her words, while the chief and elders withdrew to discuss all this. When they returned they announced their conclusion. One of the elders, Lutie Abudu, said, "I greet you heartily. Come and visit us and teach us God's words."

And Margrit did come. With the villagers, she climbed the mud steps to the top of one of the houses, and there they talked about God's words.

From the beginning, Lutie listened carefully. Later he said, "The religion of the Muslims never spoke to me, but when you spoke about Christ, I knew immediately that this was the right way to believe."

The little group in Lutie's village prospered under his leadership. He and his friends composed hymns based on the Scriptures, and these lively hymns, accompanied by joyful clapping, became an integral part of the worship services.

When Margrit went to Switzerland on furlough, she wondered what would happen to Lutie and his little group. Would they continue to meet? Would they use their one duplicated copy of Mark and the cassette recordings of Gospel stories? Was Lutie's new faith mature enough to keep the others encouraged?

The answer to all her questions was "Yes." Lutie stood firm, and the group continued to meet. Lutie's eyesight, already poor, deteriorated further so that he could not read the copy of Mark, but he listened to the recorded stories time after time, explaining what he learned to others. Having tasted the sweetness of God's Word, he began to memorize the Bible stories he could no longer read.

Sometime later, another child was born to Lutie and he decided the child should have a Christian naming ceremony. Instead of pouring out a libation to the spirits and asking them for protection of the child, he would ask God to take care of his little one.

The ceremony took place on a rooftop. As the Christians sang their hymns, the Sisaala words and characteristic Sisaala rhythms drifted out over the hot still air in the village. One man read a Scripture portion. Then, taking the child in his arms, he asked God's blessing on the young life. The ceremony demonstrated to all the village that Lutie wanted his family to follow Christ.

Over the years, Lutie's faith has been tested repeatedly. Two of his children died from measles and another died from a snake bite. But his faith has not wavered and he still shepherds the little group that meets in his village. Though his eyesight is dim, Lutie's faith is a strong light in

Mark 10:45 in Sisaala

Nibibinno bie wu kue mak
bhaa ku tumu mɛ, u kuo luu
ni tuɔnara mɛ ka suwɛ a
lɛrki la nibiino nyunne a
tuɔlaw hĩẽso.

*For even the Son of Man did
not come to be served, but to
serve, and to give his life as a
ransom for many.*

*Lutie Abudu (far left) is a
leader. He was a village
elder before he met Christ.
Now he shepherds the group
of believers that meets in his
village. Poor eyesight
prevents him from reading
God's Word, but his faith*

*stands firm as he listens to
cassette tapes, memorizes
Scripture and shares what he
learns with others.*
　　*Though not a native
Sisaala speaker, Justin
Frempong (below) became
interested in the 80,000*

*Sisaala people in 50 villages
across northern Ghana. His
involvement grew to include
literacy work, translation
and marriage. Now he leads
the Ghana Institute of
Linguistics, Literacy and
Bible Translation.*

the spiritual darkness about him.

After two years in the Sisaala work, Margrit's partner, Gertrud Sopp, moved on to another ministry. She was replaced by Regina Blass, who, like Gertrud, was from Germany.

By the time Regina joined Margrit, Justin Frempong was already becoming interested in the Sisaala people.

Justin Frempong: Called to the Sisaala

Ten days among the Sisaala people in 1969 was an exciting experience for Justin, a young university student on vacation. His home and school in southern Ghana seemed so very far away; it was almost as if he were in another world. No one here understood Twi, his mother tongue; and English, his second language, was not worth much more. The culture was also very different from anything he had ever been exposed to.

Nevertheless, Justin and his student companion learned enough about the Sisaala alphabet, which was based on a scientific analysis of the phonetic system, to be able to help people practice reading in Sisaala. They also visited many homes and, through an interpreter, told people about Christ.

Justin's visit to the Sisaala was an outgrowth of his participation in a prayer group at the University of Accra. As he listened to various speakers and read missionary biographies, he became aware of his responsibility to share Christ on his campus and in his country as a whole.

In 1969, Justin and some friends went to northern Ghana on a mission outreach. They taught Scriptures in the schools, preached in the villages

and sold Christian books in the city of Tamale.

While in Tamale, Justin learned of the Bible translation work being done among the ethnic minorities of northern Ghana. Shortly thereafter, he found himself in a Sisaala village teaching reading, struggling to learn a few Sisaala greetings, and becoming very impressed by the importance of the Bible translation task.

"The Bible meant so much to me in my own Christian walk," Justin said, "that it was obviously right to give it to others who did not have it."

Justin graduated from the university still praying earnestly about his future. When the answer came, it was a challenging one! He felt God's leading to a teaching position in northern Ghana. That meant leaving his family — not an easy thing for him to do since he was an eldest son in a culture where the eldest son is expected to shoulder heavy family responsibilities. Nevertheless, he accepted the teaching position and moved north.

One of the side benefits of Justin's new career was the closeness to the Sisaala people, whom he visited during his vacation periods, sharing the Gospel and helping people learn to read and write.

By then, Justin had picked up a little of the language and his interest in Bible translation was growing. He was beginning to sense that God wanted him to play some part in the Bible translation task.

His interest in Margrit was also growing, and in 1972, he wrote Margrit, asking her to marry him.

Margrit was shocked! She had never considered Justin in this light. After praying about it, she told Justin, "I think the Lord wants me to remain single." Nothing more was said of marriage and

the two continued their brother-sister relationship.

As the months passed, Justin's call to the Bible translation task became clearer. He decided to gain more experience in the Sisaala literacy program and then take SIL linguistic training in England during the summer of 1974.

Not long before he left, Margrit, burdened by a number of concerns, went away to spend 10 days alone with the Lord. As she was praying, the Lord brought to mind Justin's need for a wife. Suddenly God seemed to say, "You are the one for Justin." She was caught as much off guard as when she had received Justin's written proposal. She had put the idea of marriage completely out of her mind, and now here it was again. Bowing her head, she said, "Lord, if this is of You, I'll trust You to confirm it."

One evening soon after that, she met Justin at the village well and told him what had happened. Knowing that Justin did not make decisions quickly, she expected him to pray about it a long time. To her amazement, Justin came back the next evening and told her that God had already confirmed it to him — they would marry!

Justin went to SIL in England and came back as the first African member of Wycliffe Bible Translators and the Summer Institute of Linguistics. A week later he and Margrit were married. God had forged a unique partnership to see that the Sisaala people received the Scriptures.

When the newlyweds returned to the Sisaalas, Margrit continued with translation, while Justin concentrated on learning the language and directing the literacy program. By 1978 Justin was dividing his time between literacy and translation.

Literacy Day

It was Literacy Day among the Sisaalas — a day to honor those who had learned to read their own beautiful language.

"By mid-morning," Justin recounts, "people had arrived from several villages. We gathered in front of the chief's large compound. The Paramount Chief of the Sisaalas himself was the chairman, ready with a speech to encourage all to learn to read. The excited and colorful crowd vibrated with expectation and happy chatter.

"As each graduate of the reading program received his certificate from the representative of the Ghana Social Welfare and Community Development Department, a crescendo of applause arose.

"Prizes were given for the best readers and two outstanding villages received large kerosene lamps. All volunteer teachers received blue or green T-shirts with the words 'Let's read Sisaala' emblazoned on them in bold letters.

"The rhythm of the drums and the swaying of the dancers gave the day a festive flavor. After all, there was much to celebrate! One hundred twenty people had gained a significant skill — the ability to read and write in their own Sisaala language."

Sisaala Scriptures: Something Worth Reading

Month by month and year by year, the translation of the Scriptures went on. As Edwin Bawine, the main translation assistant for the Frempongs once said, "Translation is really a tedious work. You have to crack your brain to think of the words you need." But he hastened to add, "I like the work and I do it from the bottom of my heart."

Though troubled by poor health and onchocerciasis (river blindness), Edwin had a natural ability for language work. In addition to helping in the translation process, Edwin helped compile a dictionary, taught people to read and typed the final revision of the entire New Testament manuscript. Today he is helping to produce a Sisaala newspaper designed to encourage people to use their new reading skills.

One of those who helped check the translation was Samson Braima. Samson says, "Sometimes the meaning was hidden. We looked for ways to make the translation really clear to those who did not know anything about Christianity." Having helped to make the Scriptures understandable, this enthusiastic young man used them frequently to explain Christianity to his friends and his Muslim parents.

The long years of effort are now over; the Sisaala New Testament has just been completed. As it makes its way into the hands of the Sisaala people, Margrit and Justin expect God to use it mightily. They pray that the 400 readers will become many thousands of readers, and that the little groups of struggling believers will become strong, thriving churches.

Margrit recalls the day years ago when Lutie Abudu read the first words of Scripture in his language. "I watched him read each verse and think about it carefully," says Margrit. "As God revealed the meaning to him, his face would light up and he would explain it to the people around him. I never explained those Scriptures to him. It was the Holy Spirit who revealed their meaning." She anticipates others responding to their first glimpse of Scripture in the same way.

Justin is now director of the Ghana Institute of Linguistics, Literacy and Bible Translation. The young man who once stood on the sidelines of the Sisaala work is now responsible for the work in 20 language groups in his native land. Justin says, "There are many good things one can give to people, things that just meet physical needs, but God's Word gives both physical and spiritual benefit. God's Word will endure when everything else is gone."

THE PACIFIC

The Pacific Ocean — so named by explorer Ferdinand Magellan for its steady and gentle winds — today is home to 22 million people speaking a total of more than 1,000 languages.

The Pacific Area includes Australia, New Zealand, Papua New Guinea (the eastern end of the island of New Guinea) and several thousand smaller islands. It covers over 3,000,000 square miles.

The islands of the Pacific were some of the first areas to be evangelized at the beginning of the modern Protestant missionary movement — missionaries first landed in Tahiti in 1796. Papua New Guinea, one of the last great pioneer mission fields, now has one of the highest percentages of Christian believers of any nation in the world.

Papua New Guinea is the largest SIL field project. So far, linguistic work has begun among nearly 200 of its more than 600 language groups. One of these is the Barai who, like many of the Pacific peoples, have a healthy self-respect and a desire to shape their own future. SIL teams have worked among the Barai since 1968, doing linguistic studies and Bible translation and encouraging the Barai in their efforts to seek solutions to their problems.

Australia is home for about 70 groups of Aboriginal people living in its harsh "outback." The story of Ken and Lesley Hansen's work among the Pintupi illustrates some of the unique challenges and rewards that are to be found in every country and culture.

New Zealand and Australia are also significant partners in the work of Bible translation in the Pacific. Both are actively involved in recruiting and training people for the task. SIL courses have been held in Australia since 1949.

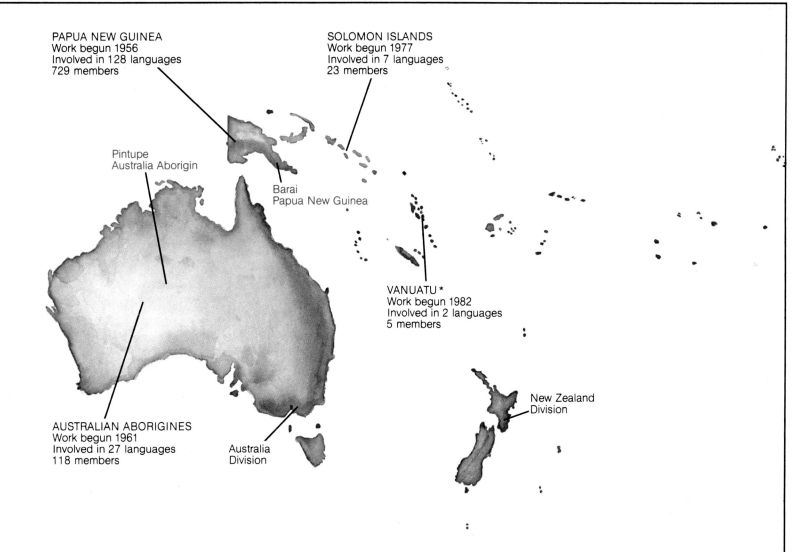

PAPUA NEW GUINEA
Work begun 1956
Involved in 128 languages
729 members

SOLOMON ISLANDS
Work begun 1977
Involved in 7 languages
23 members

Pintupe
Australia Aborigin

Barai
Papua New Guinea

VANUATU *
Work begun 1982
Involved in 2 languages
5 members

New Zealand
Division

AUSTRALIAN ABORIGINES
Work begun 1961
Involved in 27 languages
118 members

Australia
Division

*Wycliffe members serve here under auspices other than SIL.

Truly Aboriginal,
Truly Christian

The Australian outback is home for this Aboriginal girl (left). "Dreamtime" stories traditionally guided the Pintupi and other Aboriginal groups across the desert and shaped their whole approach to life. Now the Christian gospel finds expression in ancient Aboriginal art forms like this bark painting.

They walked out of the western Australian desert some 20 years ago—these hardy, resourceful Aboriginal Pintupi people. No one expected them. No one knew they were there. Over the years a few of them had appeared in Aboriginal settlements, but no one expected 800. Lured by reports of government-issued food and clothing, they left their traditional lands and the everyday fight for survival to seek a better life in the modern world.

Life in a settlement on the edge of an Australian desert would not be inviting to most people. Flies are everywhere. The daytime temperature can reach 120 degrees Fahrenheit, and the sand gets hot enough to burn your feet. When the rain comes and the cold wind blows, the temperature may drop to nearly freezing. But to the Pintupi, the food and clothing at the settlement were inviting, and the climate was normal.

For centuries these amazing people had survived on berries, dried roots, large grubs and occasional wild meat—kangaroo, emu (an ostrich-like bird) and goanna (a large lizard). They had weathered the heat and cold in brush shelters, moving from waterhole to waterhole across the trackless desert—trackless to us, that is, but not to them. From childhood they were trained to follow the "dream tracks" that crisscross the desert. They knew how to recognize the little sand and rock formations that signaled the route once taken by the "Dreamtime beings." In the early days, they believed, these creative beings—both people and animals—walked the land and shaped it. In fact, these beings actually became the landmarks in the desert. Stories of those events helped orient the Pintupi in the desert.

From childhood the Pintupi also learned to tell direction—north, east, south and west. Instead of saying "turn left," they would say "turn east" or "turn west." Later when they learned to read, they would even say, "Look at the east side of the page." Though they lived in the great outback with no apparent markers for directions, they could not fathom being lost. It just did not happen.

When the Pintupi came out of the desert, they settled close to another group of Aborigines, the Aranda, with whom Lutheran missionaries had worked. It was an Aranda leader, Obed Raggett, who married a Pintupi woman, learned her language and shared the Good News with her people.

In 1965, at the Lutherans' request, SIL translators Ken and Lesley Hansen began work among the Pintupi. They settled in Papunya, the supply depot for the Pintupi, 150 miles northwest of Alice Springs.

The Aborigines, always cautious of outsiders, were hesitant, at first, to accept the Hansens. But gradually their suspicions subsided, and they incorporated Ken and Lesley into their kinship system. They assigned Ken to a certain "skin group." Then they assigned Lesley to the skin group that should marry a person in Ken's group. By that simple act, Ken and Lesley acquired mothers and fathers, brothers and sisters; and their place in the society was settled. Now the Pintupi knew how to relate to them. Brothers would offer assistance, mothers-in-law would avoid them, and life could go on smoothly.

The Pintupi taught the Hansens how to grind seeds into powder between two stones and make a gritty brown loaf called "damper" to bake in the coals. They taught them to eat the large fatty insect larvae called witchity grubs and other "delicacies." They told them stories of the "Dreamtime" and helped them understand their deep attachment to the land—much of which they considered sacred because of the Dreamtime events which had taken place on it. As Ken and Lesley became comfortable in the language and culture, they began Bible translation and literacy work, and the Pintupi worked along with them.

Ten years after beginning translation work, Ken and his able Pintupi co-workers completed the New Testament. They then went on to translate one-third of the Old Testament. By this time they had changed the name of the translation to Pintupi-Luritja to include speakers of a closely related language.

On May 2, 1982, some 1,500 people gathered at Papunya to thank God for His Word in Pintupi-Luritja—the New Testament published by the Australian Bible Society and the abridged Old Testament by the Lutheran Church. Lutheran officials, government representatives, SIL members, Aranda, Pintupi and Luritja—all rejoiced together. A Pintupi choir sang praises to God in their language. Two Aborigines were ordained into the Lutheran ministry, adding a special touch to the dedication service.

A Pintupi named Tjakamarra Fred West gave

one of the speeches. He reminded everyone of the valuable partnership between the Hansens and the Pintupi when he said, "Together we have worked on God's Word."

Another of Ken's faithful co-workers, Tjampu Tjakamarra, said, "I want to tell you that I was reading God's Word in English and in Aranda, and I couldn't hear it. Now I clearly hear God's Word and I have believed ... and the old people and the young people, they are believing God's Words, too."

It is not easy for an Aboriginal to believe; it is all so foreign. Everything they have ever learned has been taught directly by an older person. Learning from books is not part of their culture, yet God's Word is a book. They are also tied very closely to their land, and it is hard for them to understand why Jesus, who did not walk their land or play a part in their mythology, should be important to them.

On the other hand, some aspects of their culture do prepare them for the Christian message. For instance, their interest in the beginnings makes the book of Genesis intriguing. Their mythology does not account for the creation of the earth or the Dreamtime beings who they way put the finishing touches on creation; it simply assumes their presence at the beginning. For many, recognizing God as Creator is the starting point for their belief.

The Pintupi are also peculiarly adept at understanding eternity. Their Dreamtime is not just in the past; it is past and present and future. It is "everytime," much like our "everywhere." They are not troubled, as we are, over Scriptures that say that God, from the beginning of time, knew us in Christ and chose us. They are not bound to time, as we are, but live in the "eternal now."

God's Spirit is moving among the Pintupi. In fact, whole families are deciding to follow Christ. But the growth of the church is not without stress. As the people read the Scriptures, they see that some of the teaching provides a contrast to the traditional Aboriginal mythology. Some of their old ways of thinking must change. On the other hand, some of their traditional beliefs and practices can be used effectively in worshipping God. They need wisdom to understand the difference.

Aboriginal groups have traditionally gathered for song and dance festivals, called *corroborees*, at which they have acted out Dreamtime stories. Recently speakers of several other Aboriginal languages have held Christian *corroborees*, acting out the Easter story and other biblical accounts. These graphic presentations have had a tremendous impact on the Aborigines.

Can the Pintupi, like these other groups, use *corroborees* to worship God? What form should their church services take? What is truly Aboriginal and truly Christian? These are the questions facing them.

One of the places where the answers are being sought is in Kintore, 150 miles west of Papunya. This is the new home — on traditional Pintupi land — of 300 Pintupi people. These people longed for greater control of their own community, away from other Aboriginal groups. They also saw what alcoholic beverages and other vices of "civilization" were doing to their people and decided to leave it behind.

They took with them the Scriptures and an evangelist, Smithy Tjampitjinpa. From the beginning, Smithy held daily meetings, teaching his people the Scriptures and hymns. Smithy says, "When I read this Word to them, every eye is on me. They want to hear more. Sometimes they listen and become sad because they know they have not followed God's way."

Other Christians have come to support Smithy, and their witness is bearing fruit. More than 100 people were baptized recently in a four-hour service of baptism and communion. The entire service, as well as the preparatory teaching, was organized and conducted by Aboriginal pastors and evangelists.

God's Spirit is at work in Pintupi hearts, using His Word to build a beautiful addition to His Church. He is not finished yet, but when He is, we can be sure it will be truly Aboriginal and truly Christian.

Learning to Think Like an Aborigine

Bible translators are learners. In the two sections that follow, Ken Hansen tells some of the things he discovered during his years among the Pintupi.

In 1966 when my wife and I were newlyweds, we went to live among the Pintupi people. We lived in a small caravan, or trailer house, on the edge of the Aboriginal camp, just west of the European settlement of Papunya.

The Pintupi were semi-nomadic, though they never moved too far from their supply depot at Papunya. They lived in small shelters called *humpies* made of canvas or corrugated iron piled on wood frames. Whenever anyone in the camp died, they would move on to another waterhole. When that happened, we hitched up our trailer and moved with them.

Living in such close proximity to another culture was difficult, but this was the best way for us to learn the language. We knew that the more Aboriginal activities we were involved in, the faster we would learn.

And we did get involved. In those early days, few Pintupi people had cars, and they frequently asked us to take them hunting and food gathering. Learning to eat witchity grubs and kangaroo meat that was less than well done were only some of our many memorable experiences.

At first, our progress in learning Pintupi was slow. The language had no written form, no pronunciation guides, not even an alphabet. Before we could pronounce or write a sound, we had to hear it. We often asked the people to repeat words over and over while we tried to grasp the new sounds. Sometimes the differences seemed small to us. A slight difference in tongue position was all that distinguished "lying" *(ngarrinpa)* and "standing" *(ngarinpa)*. The same was true of "talk" *(wangka)* and "alive" *(wanka)*.

Once we could hear the sounds, we had to train our tongues to pronounce them. That, too, was a challenge. We made many mistakes and often joined others in laughing at our inadequate efforts.

Trying to remember the strange combinations of sounds and words was difficult, but a greater challenge was learning to use them in the correct social situations. Everyone in an Aboriginal community has a kinship relation to everyone else. Specific rules, though unwritten, define how a person may talk to various relatives.

We did not really fit into the community until we were assigned a place in their kinship system. Then suddenly we had mothers and fathers, brothers and sisters, and an established position in the community. We also had the obligation to learn how to treat each relative.

We learned that when one was sitting in camp with a particular relative, there were certain subjects that were polite to discuss and others that

Finding the Keys

were not. This was a real dilemma for us.

We found that with some relatives it was perfectly acceptable to sit silently without conversing. It took us a while to be at ease with this since it was not a practice we had grown up with. We often felt we had to say something — anything — to keep the other person from feeling uncomfortable.

We also learned it was acceptable to joke with only certain relatives. A man's mothers-in-law's son from his own generation could be treated lightly without being offended, but members of one's parents' generation had to be treated seriously, without any joking. With other relatives, like mothers-in-law, we found we should have limited social contact. It took us a long time to learn when and to whom we should address our questions.

Early in our program, we made a list of long-term goals: analyze the grammar, create an alphabet, compile a dictionary, produce and publish primers, teach people to read, translate and publish an abridgment of the Old Testament and, of course, translate and publish the New Testament. As we lived our lives among the people, however, we discovered these goals were much easier to write than to accomplish. We often felt discouraged when we had to defer our long-range goals while we learned the language.

Nevertheless, we knew why we were there. No language communicates to the Aboriginal heart like his mother tongue, especially where difficult, non-cultural spiritual concepts are concerned. We also knew the Aborigines would need access to the truths of Scriptures in their own language if they were to handle their own church development. We wanted to see that happen.

As we lived among the Pintupis, we were constantly alert for new words and new ways to use old words. Some of the people were especially adept at helping us learn. One of these was Johnny Yangkatja Tjapurrula. When I did not understand a word or phrase, he would suggest a variety of situations in which the word could be used. Sometimes when we went hunting on Saturday, he would use a complicated grammatical construction he knew I did not understand. He would say it slowly, and then in the context of the real-life situation I would often catch on.

As time went by, we knew we would never be completely like the Pintupis, but we were beginning to see things from their point of view and beginning to think the way they thought, and that made us much more comfortable in their environment. Later, as our children were born, they were accepted as locals and, like us, felt at ease in the shelters of their Pintupi "relatives." And then it was time to begin a new chapter in our work: Bible translation.

After five years of studying the Pintupi language, we were able to communicate well enough to begin Scripture translation. Several Aborigines learned to translate along with us. We began with the Gospel of Mark. This, the shortest Gospel, is basically narrative material and thus easier to translate than other parts of Scripture.

One of our first struggles was over "key terms" — terms that are important to the biblical message but are not, in many cases, part of the Aboriginal culture. While some of these terms had already been adequately translated during the course of the Pintupis' contact with the Lutheran mission, many others had not.

After much discussion and experimentation, we found words and phrases that expressed the biblical meaning of the various terms in Aboriginal forms. "Angel," for instance, was "the one who belongs in the sky" (*nganka ngurrara*). "Pharisee" was "a teacher of the Jew's law" (*tjuwuku luwuku mikunytju*). "King" became "big boss" (*mayutju pulka*).

Deciding on the word for "God" was difficult. An earlier suggestion was "Dreaming" (*Tjukurrpa*). "Dreaming" means a creative force or forces, usually personified in people or animals. It comes out of the Aboriginal myths that describe the early days, or "Dreamtime," when creative beings walked the land and shaped it. We considered using this term and teaching the people the Christian meaning of the word. Instead, we eventually chose "One who pertains above" (*Katutja*), and time has proved it to be the correct choice.

One of my Christian Aborigine friends recently

For the Hansens, part of learning to think like an Aborigine was adapting to their semi-nomadic ways. Whenever anyone in the camp died, the people moved on to another waterhole, and the Hansens moved with them (left).

Both Ken (below) and his wife, Leslie, spent hour upon hour conversing with the people – finding out how they did things, why they did those things, and how they viewed the world. Everything the Hansens learned made them better able to fit into the Aboriginal way of life and better prepared to translate the Scriptures in a way that made sense to the Aboriginal heart.

told me, "God is not dreaming (*tjukurrpa*), he is real (*yilta*). He is before all the dreamings."

Since then I have heard people say about a Bible story, "This story is real, not a dreaming happening." While most consider the Dreamtime myths to be true, they distinguish between historical happenings and Dreamtime happenings. We are grateful we chose a term that places God in the realm of historical, real happenings, rather than the world of the Dreamtime.

During my early years in Central Australia, a missionary who had learned a little of an Aboriginal language once told me it was impossible to translate Scriptures into that language. "There are certain concepts," he said, "that simply could not be expressed in that language."

As I look back on the conversation, I realize that he knew of no way to translate other than the literal approach. In a strictly literal approach, the translator tries to find a word in the Aboriginal language to match every word in the Hebrew or Greek. Nouns are translated into nouns, verbs into verbs, and not even the word order of the sentence is disturbed. This results in an awkward style, loss of meaning and in many cases, complete nonsense.

When Martin Luther was translating the Bible into German in the 1500's, he also faced the problem of literal versus idiomatic translation, although he did not use those terms. Should he translate literally — that is, word by word from Greek or Latin into German — even if the result were awkward and meaningless? Or should he translate idiomatically — that is, by determining the meaning of the original language and then putting that meaning into good German?

Luther chose to translate idiomatically. "We do not have to inquire of the literal Latin how we are to speak German," he wrote. "... Rather we must inquire ... of the mother in the home, the children on the street, the common man in the marketplace. We must be guided by their language, the way they speak, and do our translating accordingly. That way they will understand it and recognize that we are speaking German to them."*

Similarly, when we translated the Word of God into Pintupi, we did not ask the literal structure of the Greek how we should speak Pintupi. Rather we inquired of the mother in the camp, the children playing on the track and the man sitting under a shade tree. We put the meaning of the Greek and Hebrew Scriptures into clear, natural Pintupi, and they have understood God's message.

It is perhaps even more important to translate Scripture idiomatically for the Aborigines than it is for you and me. The English language and culture is solidly based on the Greco-Roman culture, which in turn was influenced by Judaism. We can understand a literal translation far better than the Aborigines, whose language and culture have very little in common with the Biblical cultures.

Matthew 5:2 demonstrates the dangers of a literal translation for the Pintupi. In English it says, "And he opened his mouth, and taught them, saying ..." If this were translated literally, the Pintupi would understand it to mean, "Jesus opened someone else's mouth," much as a dentist would open an unwilling patient's mouth. They would also think that Jesus said something to the people before He opened His mouth and taught. In other words, "He opened his (someone else's) mouth and taught them, having said (something)."

When translated idiomatically, the meaning of the original is retained even though it sounds a bit different: "With the intention of teaching them, he was speaking like this ..."

Genesis 3:7 is another example: "And the eyes of them both were opened (and they knew that they were naked)...." With no passive form in Pintupi, "were opened" has to be changed to "He opened" or "God opened." But if we said "God opened their eyes," the Pintupi would understand the passage to mean that He opened the eyes of another two besides Adam and Eve — maybe two of the animals.

Once we had straightened that out, we would be left with the idea that God opened Adam and Eve's eyes so they could see. The Pintupi do not understand "opening someone's eyes" to mean causing them to understand. But they do have an expression "to open the ear," which means to cause someone to understand a previously hidden truth. Since this is just what the Hebrew figure of speech means, an accurate translation involves substituting "ears" for "eyes."

The idiomatic — and meaningful — translation of the verse is: "And God opened their ears...." That is, "God caused them to suddenly understand (that they were naked)...."

It will also be readily seen that accurate exegesis is extremely important for idiomatic translation. Paul and other biblical writers communicated their message as clearly and carefully as their language would allow. It is our responsibility to figure out what they meant to say and to communicate their thoughts just as clearly to the Pintupi.

*From: Luther, Martin, "On Translating, an Open Letter." *The Works of Luther*, Volume V, 1931. Holman and Company and Castle Press, Philadelphia, PA.

118

Genesis 1:1 in Pintupi
Kurralka pana yilkari
pankara Katutjalu
palyalkitjangka kuwarripa
ngarama.
*In the beginning God
created the heaven and
the earth.*

*Sitting on the ground that is
so much a part of them, these
Pintupi men (below) listen
as one of their own
expounds the Word of God
("the One who pertains
above") in their own
language.*

*OVERLEAF: Paintings took
the place of books in
traditional Aboriginal
culture. This one, rich in
symbols, tells a Dreamtime
story that any Aboriginal
could read. All paints are
homemade with pigments
from various types of plant
products and soils.*

Pintupi Kinship

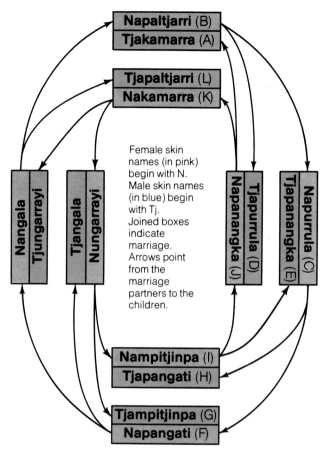

Female skin names (in pink) begin with N. Male skin names (in blue) begin with Tj. Joined boxes indicate marriage. Arrows point from the marriage partners to the children.

The skin names in the chart:

Napaltjarri (B) / Tjakamarra (A); Tjapaltjarri (L) / Nakamarra (K); Nangala / Tjungarrayi; Tjangala / Nungarrayi; Napanangka (J) / Tjapurrula (D); Napurrula (C) / Tjapanangka (E); Nampitjinpa (I) / Tjapangati (H); Tjampitjinpa (G) / Napangati (F)

T he Australian Aborigines have complex kinship systems that define who marries whom and how each individual interacts with others. Although each language group has its own kinship terms, many share basically the same system and the relationships are recognized across language boundaries. A person may travel halfway across Australia, enter a new community and find "relatives" who readily accept him into the family circle.

The kinship systems are based on "skin groups." To illustrate, the accompanying chart shows the Pintupi kinship system, which has eight "skin names" for girls and eight more for boys. Each person's skin name is determined by the skin names of his father and mother.

Appropriate marriages are indicated by the joined boxes. Arrows point to the skin names of the sons and daughters of each union.

In many ways, a man is considered the son of all who belong to the skin groups of his biological parents. He calls them all "father" and "mother" and fulfills the responsibilities of a son toward them. The same is true of other relationships. Because age has nothing to do with the relationship, mothers and fathers are often younger than their sons or daughters.

When Ken and Lesley Hansen settled among the Pintupi, the people conferred upon Ken the skin name, "Tjakamarra" (letter A on the chart). He was henceforth known as Ken Tjakamarra. Since the preferred wives for Tjakamarras are women in the Napaltjarri group (B), Lesley was assigned that name. When their daughters, Jennifer and Sharon, were born, they automatically belonged to the Napurrula group (C). Their son Keith was a Tjapurrula (D).

If Jennifer and Sharon were to marry within the system, they would marry Tjapanangkas (E). Their daughters would be Napangatis (F), their sons-in-law Tjampitjinpas (G), their sons Tjapangatis (H) and their daughters-in-law Nampitjinpas (I).

If Keith were to marry within the system, he would marry a Napanangka (J). His daughters would be Nakamarras (K) and his sons Tjakamarras (A) like his father. And so it goes.

When consultant Dave Hargrave came to stay with the Hansens to check their translation, the Pintupi made him a Tjapaltjarri (L). That made him Lesley's brother, an appropriate relationship for someone living in the same house with Ken and Lesley.

Papua New Guinea, The ABC's of Cooperation

You cannot get too far into a discussion of Papua New Guinea without realizing a juxtaposition of contrasts — steaming swamps and rain forests, shining beaches and snow-powdered mountains, and airstrips more common than roads.

Papua New Guinea is an ancient region embracing a new nation — a nation in transition from the Stone Age to the twentieth century. It is a nation where clan allegiances vie with national identity, and public officials with a wide range of educational backgrounds govern a country in which 85 percent of the people live in remote villages.

Approximately one-seventh of the world's languages are found in Papua New Guinea. Its three million people are divided into more than 700 language groups. Once known for tribal warfare and headhunting, these diverse people now enjoy a peaceful coexistence. Tolerance and adaptability are the hallmarks of the Papua New Guineans.

Witness the *lingua franca: Tok Pisin* is an adaptation of some seven languages. If a man wants to hire a worker, he hangs out a sign: *gat wok*. If he is not hiring: *nogat wok*. Simple!

The Summer Institute of Linguistics is taking a holistic approach to its work in this rapidly developing country. It is encouraging tribal groups to discover their own needs and find ways to meet those needs. SIL personnel, rather than telling villagers how to do things, stand ready to serve as facilitators and resource people.

The Barai people, for example, are a group of 2,000 subsistence gardeners and hunters who live in 17 villages in the southeastern foothills between Popondetta and Port Moresby. The Barai

were eager to create their own program. Translators Mike and Donna Olson and literacy workers Peter and Bev Evans helped Barai leaders design a project that would aid the villagers spiritually, socially, physically, and economically.

The Barai Nonformal Education Association (BNEA), now boasting 50 Barai workers, identified seven areas of development for their community: translation, literacy, Christian education, women's education, publications, short courses and support projects.

Simon Savaiko, the BNEA manager, is a zealous young Christian who has a deep concern for his people. While attending Sydney Missionary Bible College in Australia, he was impressed by the sharing/caring family atmosphere of the community church he attended. He determined to encourage that quality in the Barai churches.

Simon works around the clock serving the community. When visitors ask him what they can do for the Barai people, Simon replies, "Pray that my people will come to know the Lord in a true way and not just attend church out of habit. I want to see my people be more than nominal Chris-

tians!" This attitude permeates the BNEA programs.

The BNEA staff have realized the key to their community-assessed needs is literacy. In order to grow spiritually and socially, in order to acquire skills, in order to merge into the national life, people must be able to read. Thus, literacy is the strongest emphasis of the BNEA, with over 30 teachers and three supervisors involved in the project. Approximately 200 students attend preschool and adult literacy classes. Certificates of completion are issued, and most "graduates" join reading clubs. Courses in letter writing and mathematics are also taught.

The Barai translation effort is led by Brian Kasira, a Barai speaker. Brian once had a dream in which he heard God say, "If you are not doing in this world what you were born for, then why were you born?" Soon after that, he felt God calling him to Bible translation for his own people. Brian attended the National Translators' Course at the SIL center in Ukarumpa and began

Young adult teachers take responsibility for encouraging older Barai men and women in literacy (far left).

Though no roads lead into the Barai area (left), enthusiastic young men opened a trade store to help support the educational program.

Children work hard to make their letters neat. They look forward to graduation and the use of their new skills.

The Barai Nonformal Education Association is a total program for self-improvement. The rain tank (far left) provides a new method for washing dishes and obtaining good drinking water in the dry season.

Help is provided by installing a hydraulic ram pump for bringing water to higher levels in the village (left).

The mimeograph machine in the Barai village reproduces reading materials for the surrounding area (below right).

Like children the world over, one of this girl's favorite subjects in the educational program is hopscotch (below left).

translation work along with the Olsons.

Commenting on the literacy and translation programs, Peter Evans says, "It is a tremendous thrill to see God's Word going into the language, knowing that the people will be able to read it and understand what it is saying!"

Dovetailing with the literacy and translation programs is the Christian education project. Six Barai Bible study leaders travel from village to village holding classes. One young teacher leads Bible classes six nights a week. Said one elderly student, "When the Bible is read in another language, we don't take much notice of it. But this is in our own language and we really notice."

Bev Evans has actively assisted in the area of women's education. She has trained teachers in sewing techniques, health care and cooking. Their interest in bread baking led to the area's first oven. A 44-gallon (55-gallon U.S.) drum was insulated with rocks and dirt and equipped with a tin can smokestack. A door and rack were installed, and a fire pit was built underneath. Soon the women were not only baking bread for their families but selling some to finance their other projects.

The women have also experimented with new recipes using local foods. The recipes are being made into a cookbook which is intended not only to improve nutrition but to stimulate interest in reading.

129

The Barai people continue to enjoy their traditional clothing for special occasions. Like people anywhere, the Barai are always ready for a celebration (below).

Bev Evans (right) has a full load, teaching the Barai women sewing and nutrition as well as taking care of her own family. Part of her duties include teaching her younger

children, who are not attending school at the SIL center.

Their house (lower right) often serves as a gathering place for the whole village.

Peter comments, "We need to develop an attitude of 'literateness' so the people will make reading and writing a part of their everyday lives."

As that "literateness" spreads, the demand for reading material increases. The BNEA publications department is kept busy producing booklets, a monthly newspaper and other materials requested by various departments of the BNEA.

The short course department is exactly that: it offers short courses designed to meet specific highly desired needs, such as mechanics and bookkeeping. This department is often assisted by various individuals and government agencies from outside the Barai area.

The BNEA constantly looks for ways to support itself. One successful project, which is also a service to the community, is a trade store that sells paper, pencils, pens, Scripture portions and household goods.

A large community center was completed in 1983. Built almost entirely from local materials, it houses the offices of the BNEA departments as well as a library, the trade store and classrooms. The construction of the impressive two-story structure was a community effort. The center encourages interaction between the departments and stimulates further community participation.

Visitors to the Barai area of Papua New Guinea often comment on the way the *kunai* grass, with its tall stems crowned with puffs of fluffy seeds, sways in the breeze like ocean swells; it seems to move to a silent beat. So, too, does the nation. While many countries only dream about it, Papua New Guinea truly is an emerging nation. Her people are in motion, and SIL has played an appreciated role as facilitators of that progress.

EUROPE

The period of renaissance and reformation spanning the fourteenth to seventeenth centuries marked Europe's transition from medieval to modern society. A flowering of the arts, literature and science characterized this period. Scripture translation flourished as well. Translations by John Wycliffe, Martin Luther and others, along with the invention of moveable type, made the Bible increasingly accessible to the common people. By the end of the eighteenth century the Bible had been translated into some 34 European languages (67 worldwide).

Most of the languages of Europe now have the Bible; yet there remain a few languages spoken by smaller groups which may still need Bible translation. These include the Saam or Lapp languages of Scandinavia, Albanian and Friulian as spoken in Italy and Letzburgisch of Luxembourg. For the most part, however, the focus of Bible translation in Europe today is on the languages of those who have immigrated to Europe from their homelands around the world.

While there has been increasing translation activity on the part of Wycliffe and SIL in Europe, the primary focus of the work remains on recruiting, training and sending out translation workers to other parts of the world. Wycliffe offices operate in 14 European nations and linguistic training is available in Germany, France and England.

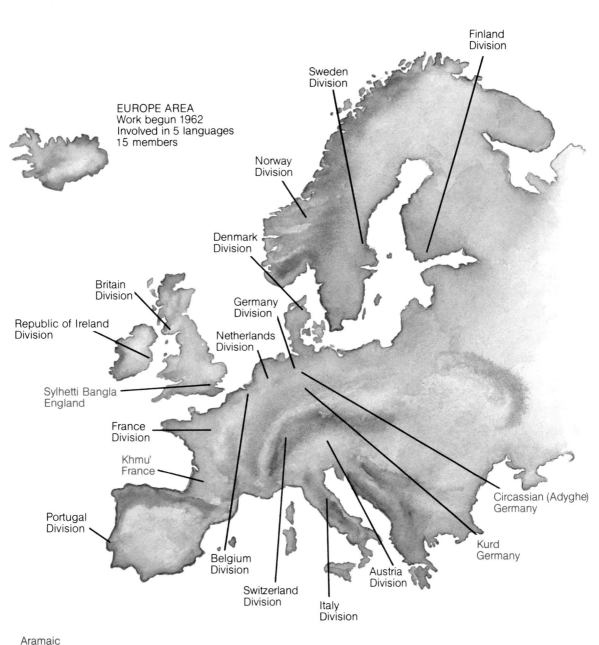

EUROPE AREA
Work begun 1962
Involved in 5 languages
15 members

Finland
Division

Sweden
Division

Norway
Division

Denmark
Division

Britain
Division

Germany
Division

Republic of Ireland
Division

Netherlands
Division

Sylhetti Bangla
England

France
Division

Khmu'
France

Circassian (Adyghe)
Germany

Portugal
Division

Kurd
Germany

Belgium
Division

Switzerland
Division

Austria
Division

Italy
Division

Aramaic
Sweden, Germany, Switzerland, Netherlands

Languages on the Move

(Right) The language of the Kurds is related to modern Persian and therefore to other European languages. The Kurds, have apparently lived many centuries within a thousand miles of Jerusalem. Still, they do not have the Bible in their language.

Traditionally, most SIL teams have left their homelands and traveled to the far corners of the earth. However, a growing number of translators, rather than going to the jungles of Amazonia or the semi-nomadic camps of desert dwellers, are going into their own backyards.

Current world turmoil — including both economic crises and armed conflict — has forced many thousands of minority language speakers to flee their native homelands. They have become refugees, immigrants and guest-workers in the United States, England, France, Germany, Israel and other countries of the free world. In a word, these are displaced peoples living outside their original homeland.

SIL teams have been at work among these groups since 1971. Currently, six displaced language projects are underway in Europe and the United States, and some New Testaments are nearing completion. Because some groups are traditionally opposed to the Gospel, overt publicity could cause difficulty for those helping SIL teams in their translation work. Prayer for these groups, however, is essential.

However we may hurt over the unsettled world conditions that caused these language groups to be displaced, there does exist today a mission opportunity that is unprecedented. On our very doorstep are peoples whose government have forbidden the work of Christian missions in their countries. Rather than feel threatened by neighbors whose language and customs are different from our own, we can recognize this as a new opportunity to reach out with Christ's love across language and culture barriers.

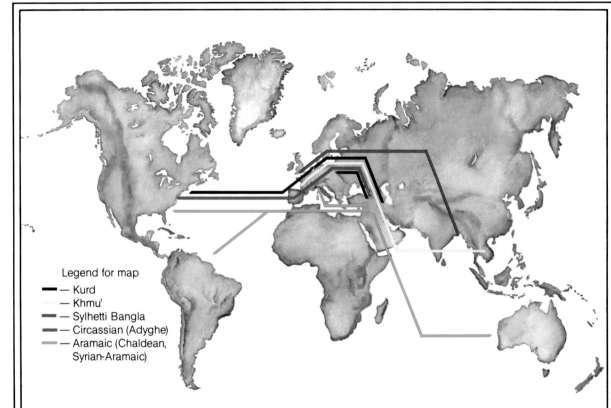

Legend for map
■ — Kurd
— Khmu'
■ — Sylhetti Bangla
■ — Circassian (Adyghe)
— Aramaic (Chaldean, Syrian-Aramaic)

The history of the world is the story of movement—people moving from one place to another in search of a better life. For centuries, political and religious oppression or economic distress have forced the migration of large groups of people. The Sylhetti left Bangladesh, a British Commonwealth country, for the hope of finding work in England. The Circassian left the Caucasus, a region east of the Black Sea, for the Middle East, Germany and the United States. Groups of Aramaic speakers from the Mesopotamian area scattered throughout Europe, Australia, and North and South America.

Today, numbers of immigrants appear to be on the rise. More than ever, this seems to be the Age of the Refugee. What follows are the stories of two fairly recently displaced groups, the Kurds of the Middle East and the Khmu' of Southeast Asia.

Many Iranian Kurds still live in these traditional clay-roofed houses of mud or stone (below). Windows are high and small, serving as smoke holes in place of chimneys. Carpets and pillows provide the basic furniture.

The Kurds, a proud and embattled minority, have struggled for the right of self-determination since 1924. This Kurdish family (right) hosted Terry Todd and a colleague when they visited Iran.

(Far right) SIL translator Terry Todd standing between a Kurdish father and son.

New Words for An Ancient People

The Kurds are an ancient people inhabiting the mountains and foothills northeast of the Tigris and Euphrates Rivers. This area, known as Kurdistan, is not a nation in the political sense, because it is divided among the nations of Iran, Iraq, Turkey, Syria and the Soviet Union. Kurds claim they have inhabited these rugged mountains for over 3,000 years and are the descendants of the Medes, conquerors of the Babylonian empire.

A few groups of Kurds are still pastoral nomads who live in goat-hair tents and drive their herds of sheep, goats and cattle to the mountains in summer and onto the plains in winter. The great majority, however, are farmers who combine agriculture with herding and live in small houses built of mud or stone. To preserve their scarce agricultural land, the Kurds cluster in small villages and towns, often on steep hillsides.

Like most peoples of the Middle East, the Kurds are Moslems. Until the end of World War I, they formed an ethnic minority within the Ottoman and Persian Empires. With the breakup of the Ottoman Empire and the formation of separate nations in the area, it would have been logical to set up an autonomous Kurdistan nation, but history passed them by. By 1924, the borders of the present-day nations were established with no mention of Kurdistan. Since that time, the Kurds have struggled to unite themselves and win some degree of autonomy.

The politics of Kurdish nationalism make it impossible to do translation work in the Kurdish homelands. For this reason, SIL translators Terry and Lynn Todd work in Germany, where approximately 250,000 Kurdish guest-workers from Turkey have settled. The Todds have located a community of 32 Kurdish families who claim to have been Christians since apostolic times. These people are eager to have the Bible in their language and have promised to help the Todds as much as possible. The Todds hope to involve Moslem groups in their translation efforts as well, so that all Kurds can feel the final product be-

longs to them.

Terry and Lynn long for the day when the Kurds might hear words like these in their own language: "I am the good shepherd; I know my sheep, and my sheep know me . . . I lay down my life for the sheep. I have other sheep that are not of this sheep pen. I must bring them also. They too will listen to my voice, and there shall be one flock and one shepherd" (John 10:14-16, NIV).

A Kurdish shepherd in Iran (below) cares for his flock. The Kurds claim to have descended from the Medes, who along with the Persians, conquered the Babylonian Empire.

(Right) For the most part, Kurds are followers of the Islamic religion. However, there are some Kurdish Christians. Translators Terry and Lynn Todd have contacted some whose Christian roots date back to before the advent of Islam. These Christians are very interested in helping with the translation.

(Far right) Thousands of Kurdish guest-workers from Turkey have settled in the villages and major cities of Germany. The Todds first began working on the Kurdish language in the U.S. with the help of Kurdish refugees from Iraq. Now they have moved to Germany and are continuing the project.

(Below right) Kurdish refugees in Dallas, Texas, dance at a Newroz (Kurdish New Year — March 21) picnic.

138

Which Script?

In modern times, Kurdish has been written in four entirely different alphabets. Armenians who knew Kurdish used an adapted form of their own alphabet. In Iran, Iraq and Syria, the Arabic script has been adapted to Kurdish. In the Soviet Union, an official Kurdish alphabet has been made from the Cyrillic alphabet used for Russian. And Kurds who have grown up in Turkey have adapted the modern Turkish alphabet, based on Latin, for writing their language.

More than 100 years ago, an entire Kurdish New Testament was printed in the Armenian script. Unfortunately, it was never used by the Kurds, and today most Kurds do not know that alphabet and are not interested in learning it. They have requested that the version currently being translated be made available in both the Arabic and Latin scripts.

ARMENIAN

Սկզբում Աստված ստեղծեց երկինքն ու երկիրը։ Գավառն թէ ու նախա վերջ մասերին հարբե երկիանաբ։

ARABIC

ميس مسيح نلك اودا نيث تابس نلك باس، پيغمبر لس
دلك باز غان منه من سنك آ لدكردن او

CYRILLIC

Кудай Улы Іисусъ Христостың Евангеліесінің басы. Байгамбарлардың жазганы: мне Мен Сенің

LATIN

Û sala panzdehemîn ya xundikarîtiya Tibaryos Qeyser de Pilatos Pontî wali- yê Cuhistanê, û Hêrodos serekê çaryekê Celîlê, û brayê wî Filîpos serekê çaryekê

139

The Khmu'— Still Waiting

Like the Kurds, the Khmu' people of Southeast Asia need the Scriptures in their own language.

In 1880, Dr. David McGilvary, an American Presbyterian missionary, arrived in Laos by elephant and began working among the Khmu' people. Repeated visits by Dr. McGilvary and his colleagues resulted in a large Christian community.

Today, the Khmu' church in Laos is growing, and there are reports of large numbers of Christians.

Ironically, these original inhabitants of Laos, the first to be evangelized, are still waiting for the Scriptures to become available in their language. Some translation work was done by Catholic priests and Khmu' speakers in the early 1960's, but most was lost or destroyed during the war and revolution. Only mimeographed copies of some passages have been preserved.

The Khmu' people have traditionally lived among speakers of other languages in Laos and other Southeast Asian countries and have assimilated well. Approximately two-thirds of them are said to be bilingual and literate in Laotian. However, the people are deeply concerned lest they lose their language. The older generation still speak Khmu' fluently, but the younger members of the community also want to learn to read and write their mother tongue.

While there is virtually no access to the more than 325,000 Khmu' speakers living in Southeast Asia, SIL has made contact with several educated Khmu' speakers who have emigrated to France. These people want to see the Scriptures in their language and are willing to help translate it.

The Khmu' translation project will probably be

a joint effort between the educated Khmu' of France and SIL translator Elisabeth Preisig, who will act as facilitator. Under this agreement, it is possible that the translation may be completed in just a few years.

However, doing the translation is one thing; getting it into the people's hands is another. Whereas it should be fairly easy to get the translated Scriptures to Khmu' speakers in countries like Thailand, it will probably be much more difficult to get them into other Southeast Asian countries. With the prayers of God's people, even this nearly impossible project can be completed.

These children (far left) are part of the Khmu' community in France. Though many of them are educated in French, they also want to retain their Khmu' language and heritage.

(Below left) Familiar status symbols surround a Khmu' boy in Thailand.
(Middle) Elisabeth visits Khmu' friends in Thailand.
(Below) More than 325,000 Khmu' speakers are scattered throughout their Southeast Asian homelands and other adopted countries. The job will not be complete until these and other Bibleless peoples have Scripture in a language they understand.

Photographers

t = top, b = bottom, r = right, c = center, l = left

Herman Aschmann — 12 r
Rodney Bartlett — 54 t, 55 l, 58, 59 l, c
Betty Blair — 13 r
Dan Bonnell — 90-91, 92, 93 (both), 94, 95, 96
    (both), 97, 98 (both), 99, 101 (both), 102, 103
    (both), 104, 105, 106, 107, 108, 109 (all)
Marjorie Buck — 26, 27, 28, 29 (both), 30-31, 32
    (both), 33, 34 (both), 35, 36, 37
Tim Burkett — 19 (all)
Dan Daniel — 5, 18, 91 r, 100
David Duncan — 6, 17 l
Kirk Franklin — 16 l, 122-123, 124 (both), 125, 126
    (both), 127, 128 (both), 129 (both), 131 (all)
David Glasgow — 116 l
Roy Gwyther-Jones — 112, 114 cl, 116, 117
Ken Hansen — 114 tl, 115, 119, 120-121
Don Hesse — 81 tr, 84 (both)
Steve Kaetterhenry — 38 tl
Alan MacDonald — 22 r
Scott Nelson — 17 r
Dave Nichols — 20, 21, 22 l, 23, 139 tl, tr
Ron Olson — 39, 40, 41 (both), 42 (all), 43, 44
    (both), 45
Elizabeth Preisig — 140 (both), 141, 142 (all), 143
Peter Silzer — 72 lb
Paul Smith — 113
Hugh Steven — 9, 48, 49 (both), 50 (both), 51,
    52 (all), 53 (both), 54 c, 55 tr, 56 (both), 57
    (both), 59 r, 62-63, 64 (both), 65, 66, 67 (both),
    68, 69 (both), 71, 72 c, 73, 74-75, 76, 77 (both)
Terry Todd — 135, 136, 137 (both), 138, 139 b
John Walton — 2-3, 17 c, 78, 79, 80, 81 l, br, 82
    (both), 83, 85 r, 86 (both), 87, 88, 89
Phil White — 14 cr
Ken Wiggers — 15

This book was set in Garamond Light by Thompson
Type, San Diego, California.
Color separations by American Color Corporation,
San Diego, California.
Printed by Graphic Arts Center, Portland, Oregon.

Wycliffe Members

The Wycliffe Bible translation movement is a team effort. The task is huge, so the team must be large. The following are the names of all Wycliffe members, listed by home country. Not included are thousands of others who are also part of the team, who stand behind members in prayer, concern, and financial support. Without these the work would not go forward.

Austria Division

Wolfgang & Erna Binder
Dora Schrotter
Wolfgang & Elfriede Stradner

Australia Division

Roger & Ruth Alder
David Andersen
Bruce & Sandra Anderson
Colin & Rosemary Anderson
Russell & Gwendoline Anderson
Marjorie Archbold
Ruby Arthur
Joy Atkinson
Richard & Rosemary Austin
Jeffrey & Valmai Bailey
Barry & Helen Baker
Roseann Barnes
John & Margaret Beaumont
Keith & Kathleen Benn
Douglas & Jeanette Bennett
Edwin & Laurel Bentley
Keith & Christine Berry
Margaret Blowers
David & Marijogen Bosma
James & Helen Boxwell
Dorothy Bradshaw
Mark & Narda Bradshaw
George & Marilyn Brady
Carl & Gaynor Brown
Gordon & Ruth Bunn
Eric & Barbara Burrows
Lynne Callinan
William & Sandra Callister
Hilary Carne
Raymond & Elizabeth Christmas
Joan Coleman
Edgar & Esther Collier
Kenneth & Margaret Collier
Lex & Valerie Collier
Martin & Elizabeth Combs
Neville & Robin Cooling
Michael Corden
Nancy Costello
Graeme Costin
Janet Cowden
Ronald & Dawn Cox
David & Janet Crawford
Lenard & Mavis Creagh
David & Ruth Cummings
Ronald & Shirley Dallinger
Robyn Davies
Rowland & Shirley Dawson
Fred & Edith Day
Victor & Grace Dean
Hank & Valerie Devries
Antonio & Valeria Di Lullo
Marinus & Geeske Doedens
John & Elizabeth Donnelly
Cheryl Duffy
Peter & Valerie Dunstan
David & Nancy Earley
Paul & Ann Eckert
Lindy Eldred
George & Wendy Elliott
Dallas & Jenny Elvery
E Leigh & Gillian Evans
Peter & Beverley Evans
Edgar & Frances Every
Bryan & Janet Ezard
Courtney & Helen Ezard
George & Susan Forman
Kirk & Christine Franklin
Margaret Garner
Elaine Geary
Brian & Helen Geytenbeek
Gwen Gibson
Clifford & Eleanor Gibson
David & Kathleen Glasgow
Warren & Jessie Glover
Marie Godfrey
Cedric & Margaret Grace
Maurice & Denese Grace
Geoffrey & Judith Grayden
Roy & Janet Gwyther-Jones
Joan Hainsworth
Kenneth & Lesley Hansen
Roma Hardwick
Dwight & Margaret Hartzler
Graham & Irene Haywood
Robert & June Head
Stephen & Jocelyn Head
Joan Healey
Alan & Phyllis Healey
James & Anne Henderson
Cornelis & Thona Herweynen
Victor & Valerie Hess
Lorraine Heywood
Thomas & Elsie Hibberd
Helen Hillas
John & Helen Hobson
Alf & Andrea Holmen
Bruce & Joyce Hooley
Frank & Janice Hoskin
Alma Hudson
Nancy Hughes
Bruce & Eula Hunt
Ian Hutchinson
Anthony & Coralie Hyett
Barry & Ruth Irwin
Raymond & Marilyn Johnston
Rodney & Lynette Jones
Rodney & Judith Kennedy
Darryl & Delwyn Kernick
Harland & Marie Kerr
Heather Kilgour
Christine Kilham
Poh San Kwan
William & Audrey Langlands
Raymond & Glenda Leach
Una Leary
Jennifer Lee
Tom & Maureen Lee
Robert & Muriel Linton
David & Daphne Lithgow
Richard & Joyce Lloyd
Ernest & Patricia Lowcock
Kenneth & Lesley Lowe
Lorna Luff
Milton Lund
Margaret Manning
Doreen Marks
James & Marjorie Marsh
Laurence & Valmai Maskell
Margaret Mathieson
Phillip & Roma Mathieson
Delle Matthews
Michael & Diane Matthews
Jean May
Kevin & Wendy May
Norman & Helen McNair
Margaret Mickan
William & Helen Miles
Philip & Shirley Mitchell
Philip & Margaret Mitton
James Morell
Win Morgan
Carol Morris
Geoff & Aileen Morrow
Beth Morton
Kevin & Wendy Nicholls
Rodney & Janny Niejalke
John & Sylvia Nowlan
Marilyn O'Connor
Desmond & Jennifer Oatridge
James & Diana Parker
Douglas & Margaret Parrington
Harold & Hazel Parsons
Audrey Payne
Jennifer Pederson
Rosemary Peeler
Marjory Perry
Arthur & Doris Pfeffer
Joan Pitt
Alison Poole
Noreen Pym
Stewart & Denise Randall
Eirlys Richards
Shirley Robertson
Muriel Rodda
Jann Russell
John & Joy Sandefur
Barbara Sayers
John & Yvonne Schatz
George & Noella Scott
Graham & Margaret Scott
Pamela Shearer
Clifford & Irene Shelton
John & Judith Simpson
Heather Sims
Rosewitha Smith
Neville & Gwyneth Southwell
David & Gladys Strange
Chester & Lynette Street
Mary Stringer
Kim Cheng & Seok Kim Tan
Doreen Taylor
Robyn Terrey
Neville & Gweneth Thomas
Susan Thompson
Annette Tomkins
Gustaff Van Der Kooij
Alexander & Lois Vincent
Annette Walker
Bruce & Glenys Waters
Pam Webb
Ross & Lyndal Webb
Thomas & Gwendoline Webb
Margaret Wells
Pamela Weston
Leonard & Margaret Whalley
Judith Wharrie
Peter & Ruth Wickham
Jennifer Williams
Anthony & Mary Williams
Eleanor Willingham
Peter & Mary Willison
Patricia Wilson
George & Faith Wilson
Raymond Wood
Kevin & Heather Woods
Lance & Margaret Woodward
Robert & Rosemary Young

Belgium Division

Robert & Clazina De Craene
Andre & Cathy De Winne
Andre & Annemarie Lanoo

Britain Division

Catherine Aberdour
Margaret Alford
Douglas & Gunnel Anderson
Mary Annett
Francis & Patricia Aze
Rachel Bale
Katharine Barnwell
William & Anne Bass
Caroline Beckley
David & Margaret Bendor-Samuel
John & Pamela Bendor-Samuel
Julie Bentinck
Joseph & Lillian Boot
Mary Breeze
Alan & Ritva Brown
Brian & Celia Bull
Stephen & Claudia Burdon
Eunice Burgess
John & Kathleen Callow
Shirley Chapman
Leonard & Amy Chipping
Heather Coates
Neville & Robin Cooling
Monica Cox
David & Elizabeth Crozier
Sheila Crunden
Paul & Jean Dancy
Herbert & Maila Davies
Philip Davison
Andre & Cathy De Winne
James & Margaret Decker
Desmond & Grace Derbyshire
Kathleen Diment
Keith & Lorraine Doust
Elizabeth Eade
Paul & Margaret Farncombe
Timothy & Joy Farrell
John & Pamela Fletcher
Betty Forshaw
Michael & Margaret Foster
Sylvia Foulds
Winifred French
Richard & Phyllis Fry
Helen Goodship
David & Trevis Gosling
Eric & Barbara Graham
Peter & Nita Grainger
Sharon Gray
Ian & Claire Gray
Ivor & Sylvia Green
Donald & Cherrill Gregson
Glyndwr & Cynthia Griffiths
Susan Hague
Joan Hall
Edward & Kathleen Hall
Keir & Gillian Hansford
Joanna Harris
June Hathersmith
Robert & Sylvia Hedinger
Jennifer Hepburn
Patricia Herbert
Philip & Judith Hewer
Kathleen Higgens
Margaret Hill
Sonia Hine
William & Jennifer Hogg
Marshall & Jean Holdstock
John & Pamela Hollman
Mary Hood
Richard & Anne Hoyle
Joyce Huckett
Jock & Katy Hughes
Geoffrey & Rosemary Hunt
Christopher & Elaine Hurst
Ralph & Maureen Ireland
Evelyn Jackson
Kevin & Susan Jarrett
Anne Jarvis
Dorothea Jeffrey
Edna Johnson
Gordon & Rosemary Jones
Lynda Kerley
Peter & Shirley Kingston
Margaret Laidler
David & Rachel Landin
Margaret Langdon
John Lees
Martin & Patricia Leigh
Stephen & Agnes Levinsohn
Margaret Linton
Ivan & Margaret Lowe
John & Jane Maire
Carol Mansell
Mary Mansfield
Margaret Manton
Robert McKenzie
Ruth McLeod
David & Irene Meech
Eleanor Melville
Andrew Mill
Valerie Mitchell
David Morgan
Kathleen Morris
Roger & Christina Mundy
Isabel Murphy
Cyril Myers
Anthony & Dianne Naden
Constance Naish
Elizabeth Olsen
Elizabeth Parker
Muriel Parrott
Brian & Rachel Parsons
Joseph & Heather Patrick
Michael & Joan Payne
Denise Perrett
Gordon & Dorothy Perrett
Mona Perrin
Andrew & Janet Persson
Jean Peters
John Phillips
Philip & Julia Pike
O Stephen Pillinger
Diane Poole
Anthony Pope
Denise Potts
Leslie & Kitty Pride
Cynthia Radden
Timothy Raymond
Joan Richards
Douglas & Hazel Rixon
John & Kwai Roberts
Clinton & Mollie Robinson
Edward & Muriel Rowland
Philip & Heather Saunders
Stephen & Janice Schooling
Stuart & A Mary Shepherd
Ronald & Margaret Sim
Pamela Slight
Myrtle Spencer
David & Nancy Spratt
David & Muriel Standing
Ronald & Llewellyn Stanford
Mary Steele
Alberta Stoaling
Gillian Story
Marjory Tagg
Maureen Taylor
John & Audrey Taylor
Peter & Daphne Taylor
Elaine Thomas
Alfred & Joy Tobler
Geoffrey & Jacqueline Tonkin
Sheila Tremaine
John & Sheila Tuggy
Tom & Esther van Aurich
Ronald & Dorothy Virrels
Irene Walker
Christine Waring
Fiona Watson
Barbara Watts
E Helen Weir
Michael Werner
Helen Wilson
Peter & Eunice Wilson
Lynn Wood
Margaret Wood
Susan Woolcott

Brazil Division

Peter & Carmosina Carlson
Helena Flor
Wilbur & Ida Pickering
Meinke Salzer
Tine Van Der Meer

Canada Division

Shirley Abbott
Clara Abma
Glen & Emily Ager
Richard & Roslyn Albright
Andre & Roselyne Amsing
Roscoe & Marianne Amy
Lynn Anderson
E Richard & Ruth Anderson
Donald & Lindy Arnot
Helen Ashdown
Frances Atkinson
John & June Austing
Eric & Ruth Barkey
Ronald & Martha Barkey
Kenneth Barsness
Rodney & Lieselotte Bartlett
Carolyn Bentley
William & Sharon Bieber
Wolfgang & Erna Binder
Alfred & Cathryn Birtles
Robert & Janet Blager
Ed & Bea Blight
Willem & Carolyn Bontkes
Ted & Cornelia Bootsma
Ralph & Dianna Borthwick
Ralph & Vera Borthwick
Helen Braun
Martha Braun
Gerald & Carol Brock
Alford & Ruby Brooks
Clifford & Janice Brown
Larry & Judith Brown
Eva Burton
Robert & Lenora Butt
James & Valerie Carleton
Robert & Ruth Chapman
Gayle Chappell
Winston & Beverly Churchill
Allen & Isabel Coates
Marie Cooper
Marion Cowan
Kenneth & Patricia Cromer
Stanley & Jean Crossley
Geert & Gelske DeKoning
James & Gladys Dean
Alfa Delgaty
Hendrik & Margreet Den Oudsten
Daniel & Susan Deyell
Sharon Dickinson
Margaret Dobson
Verna Doerksen
Audrey Dorsch
Lena Dueck
Lois Dunkley
Randy & Linda Easthouse
Rosemary Ebenal
Fraser & Dianne Edwards
Theodor & Gloria Engel
Ross & Ellen Errington
Lesley & Marianne Fast
Peter & Mary Fast
Debbie Faulkner
Larry & Sharon Fjeldstrom
George & Marilyn Folz
Murray & Joan Forbes
Velma Foreman
Keith & Wilma Forster
Philip & Janice Foster
Bernhard & Esther Friesen
Rudy Friesen
Carman Frith
Shirley Funnell
Peter & Judy Gazard
Daniel & Karen Giesbrecht
Reginald & Marilyn Giesbrecht
Vern & Vivian Goheen
Virginia Golany
Harold & Caryle Good
Lois Gordon
Karl & Winnifred Grebe
Bruce & Judith Grebeldinger
Peter & Christine Green
William & Jacoba Groot
Uwe & Elke Gustafsson
Geerten (Jerry) & Kathryn Haasdyk
Robert & Ingrid Hall
David & Elvera Hamm
Richard & Alice Harder
Wm Roy & Margaret Harrison
John & Irene Harssema
Freeman & Corine Hatch
Harold & Marilynn Haynes
Marion Heaslip
Daniel & Teresa Heath
Alan Hebbes
Vernon & Peggy Ann Hein
William & Anne Helen Helmus
Gertrude Heppner
Mary Hewitt
Robert & Marion Hills
Ann Hook
Bruce & Joyce Hooley
Paul & Elizabeth Hooper
Hope Hurlbut
Christopher & Elaine Hurst
Lillian Jakeman
Michael & Judith Johnson
James & Kiyoko Kakumasu
Randy & Ruth Kamp
Stephen & Patricia Kempf
Isabel Kerr
Keith & Yvonne Kerr
Tim & Linda Kevern
John & Laura King
Robert & Elizabeth Kirby
Heidi Klapauszak
Howard & Linda Klassen
Edward & Sally Koehn
Trevor Kokot
Abram & Debra Koop
Gordon & Lois Koop
Brenda Krabsen
Andrew & Edna Krahn
Rick & Karen Krowchenko
Marshall & Helen Lawrence
Alan & Donna Lea
Tom & Maureen Lee
Myles Leitch
Robert & Sheila Lever
Reinhold & Marjorie Liedtke
Patricia Lillie
William & Laura Locke
Beverly Loland
Peter & Bernice Lycklama
Bruce & Karen Lynn
Marjorie (Pat) MacLeod
Shirley Magri
David & Margaret Mannings
Rundell & Judith Maree
Mary Martens
Denis & Diana Masson
Blake & Donna Matthews
Eleanor McAlpine
Harry & Lucille McArthur
Richard & Carol McArthur
Joyce McCarthy
Jeffrey & Michele McGrew
Ian & Arlette McGrigg
Ruth McIntosh
Les & Ella McKellar
Paul & Alice Meisner
Harvey & Hilda Milke
James & Marion Miller
Barry & Bonita Moeckel
Victor & Anita Monus
David & Lorna Munnings
Peter & Mary Jane Munnings
Graydon & Gladys Murdock
Carol Muzzy
Beatrice Myers
Stewart & Edith Nelson
Hulda Neufeld
Leonard & Johanna Newell
John & Jeannette Newton
Dennis & Erna Newton
Raymond & Ruth Nicholson
Mark & Irene Nickel
Helena Oderkirk
Keith & Erika Palmer
Deborah Papuc
Nicolas & Dora Pauls
Wesley & Kathryn Peacock
Helen Pease
Edward & Joyce Peasgood
Telford & Claire Penfold
Thomas & Penny Phinnemore
Donald & Mary Pitman
William & Charlotte Plumer
Howard & Eunice Pole
Jack & Josephine Popjes
Jerry & Joanne Potma
Larry & Grace Rau
Roger & Marilyn Reeck
Aileen Reid
Jeanette Reimer
Martha Reimer
Viola Reimer
Richard & Sandra Reimer
Joanne Rennie
Terry Rich
Orland & Phyllis Rowan
Cecil & Wilda Rowland
Larry & Carol Sagert
Timothy & Sharon Sandvig
Louise Sawyer
Walden & Elfriede Schmidt
Horst & Eugenia Schulz
Terrelene Scruggs
Larry & Doreen Seibel
Olive Shell
Carol Sherk
Margaret Shields
Carol Simpson
Steve & Victoria Simpson
James Skelton
Richard & Laura Skonnord
Jean Smith
Elizabeth Smith
Saloma Smith
Stephen & Mathilda Smith
Keith & Ruth Snider
Darryl & Lynda-Joy Snyder
Edward & Linda Speyers
Roger & Ruth Spielmann
Carol Stanley
Hugh & Norma Steven
Dennis & Jean Stratmeyer
Robert & Verna Stutzman
Wilfried & Donna Sulz
Lois Sutcliffe
Philip & Susan Tees
Scott & Janet Thaxton
Grace Thiessen
Bernard & Heidi Thiessen
Arnold & Judith Thiessen
Rosemary Thomson
Ruth Thomson
Gregory & Angela Thomson
Roy & Rosemary Tibbit
Albert & Elizabeth Tiemstra
Edwin (Tony) & Nargis Trowbridge
Peter Twele
Alice Van Helden
Louis & Cornelia Van Nes
Richard & Shirley Walker
Robert & Mary Walker
Larry & Margaret Walrod
Michael & Verna Walrod
Lillian Ward
Alan & Iris Wares
Miriam Weber
Donald & Thelma Webster
Marlene Weins
Linda Weisenburger
Rosalind Whalley
Herbert & Hilda Whealy
Carl & Patricia Whitehead
Allan & Anne Wideman
Cornelius & Ruth Wiebe
Jacob & Sharlene Wiebe
Hartmut & Virginia Wiens
Hugo & Lydia Wiens
Mac & Marlise Wigfield
Regenald & Ivy Willems
Gary & Darlene Williams
Lloyd & Dorothy Williams
Bruce & Betty Witteveen
Sebo & Vina Woldringh
Cornelius & Doris Wolfe
Susan Wonnacott
Hazel Wrigglesworth
Samuel & Dolores Wuermli
Hugh & Gloria Yoder
Lillian Younker
Donald & Irmgard Ziemer

Cameroon Division

Joseph & Becky Mfonyam

Denmark Division

Iver & Alice Larsen

Ecuador Division

Elena Miranda Suarez

Finland Division

Richard & Kielo Brewis
Alan & Ritva Brown
Robert & Salme Bugenhagen
Juha & Pirkko Christensen
Herbert & Maila Davies
Ernst-august & Eeva Gutt
Helja Heikkinen
Ritva Hemmila
Pirjo Jantunen
Liisa Jarvinen
Marjo Karhunen
Elsa Korhonen
Carl & Ritva Lehonkoski
Katri Linnasalo
Arnold & Maija Lock
Pirkko Luoma
Katriina Makela
Johanna Manner
Tarja Olkinuora
Soini & Kaija Olkkonen
Inka Pekkanen
Mirja Saksa
Aira Suormala
Paula Tornroos
S Mirjami Uusitalo
Kari & Susanne Valkama
Olavi & Marja Vesalainen
Veli & Heli Voipio
Carl & Ritva Von Bell
Paula Vuorinen
Hans Wikstrom

France Division

Marie-Therese Courtet
Martine Ehrismann
Christian & Louise Grandouiller

Jacques & Marie-Claire Nicole
Francis Petit
Isabelle Plautz
Paul Solomiac
Rene & Phyllis Vallette

Germany Division

Sabine Aurnhammer
Rodney & Lieselotte Bartlett
Dietlinde Behrens
Hildegard Betz
Dorothea Binder
Regina Blass
Anne-ruth Bormuth
Ursula Bremicker
Ulrich & Ursula Bukies
Stephen & Claudia Burdon
Nicolaas & Annerose de Jong
Erika Decker
Peter & Gudrun Dommel
Ingeborg Egner
Erika Erkmann
Gerhard & Ruby Fast
Eva Flik
Mario & C Marina Goepfert
Fritz Goerling
Hella Goschnick
Bettina Gottschlich
Ernst-august & Eeva Gutt
Margret Haun
Lydia Hoeft
Monika Hoehlig
Andreas & Anna Holzhausen
Herbert & Tamara Horn
Ulrike Issmer
Rosemarie Jung
Lydia Krafft
Kurt & Hanna Krafft
Wolfram & Ilse Kreikebaum
Klaus & Leni Kruse
Klaus-peter & Doris Kuegler
Gertrude Kurrle
Frank & Ursula Lautenschlager
Christa Link
Anita Maibaum
Wilhelm & Ingrid Nitsch
Wolfgang & Marianne Paesler
Werner & Ingrid Riderer
Hans-josef & Ursula Rossbach
Rolf & Renata Schieber
Sonja Schloegel
Marieke Schoettelndreyer
Burkhard & Heiderose Schoettelndreyer
Hanz-juergen & Christel Scholz
Martin & Helga Schroeder
Andreas & Ulrike Schubert
Marlene Schulze
Wolf & Hildegard Seiler
Klaus & Janice Spreda
Bernhard Steiert
Richard & Johanna Steinbring
Wilfried & Annelie Stephan
Wolfgang & Elfriede Stradner
Arnd Strube
Sueyoshi & Ingrid Toba
Christa Toedter
Klaus & Charlotte Wedekind
Helga Weiss
Ursula Wiesemann
Hans-georg & Eva Will
Brigitte Woykos
Charlotte Zahn

Ghana Division

Grace Adjekum
Justin & Margrit Frempong

Indonesia Division

Nitya Ongkodharma

Japan Division

Takashi & Aiko Fukuda
Akemi Hanzawa
Kazuo & Chiyoko Hashimoto
Manabu & Eiko Ishikawa
Takashi & Kazue Manabe
Takashi & Michiko Matsumura
Yasuko Nagai
Hiroko Oguri
Yushin & Takako Taguchi
Masahiro & Yuko Takata
Isao & L Susan Tezuka
Sueyoshi & Ingrid Toba
Kiyoko Torakawa
Ritsuko Yamami

Korea Division

Jee-young & Jin-sook An
Eui-jung & Yun-hwa Kim

Mexico Division

Rodrigo & Carol Barrera
Artemisa Echegoyen
Priscila Palomino
Maria Villalobos

Netherlands Division

Johan & Geertruida Bakker
Ruurt & S Elisabeth Bakker
Wietze & Dorothy Baron
T Enoch & Bongi Bham
Sara Bijl
Corrie Boer
Albertine Bosch
David & Marijogen Bosma
Nicolaas & Pamela Daams
Martien & Attie de Groot
Nicolaas & Annerose de Jong
Hendrik & Margreet den Oudsten
Jacob & Morina Feenstra
Hilleen Fleurke
Wilhelmina Heijdanus
Rudolf & Jacoba Hidden
Anna Huiskamp
Pieter & Johanna Koen
Hanneke Korten
Alma Kroese
Emmy Kuisch
Constance Kutsch Lojenga
Fritz & Anneke Lauffenburger
Ingeborg Leenhouts
Auke & Tjitske Lemstra
Arnold & Maija Lock
Johannes & Jantine Lotterman
Frederik & Neeltje Niemeyer
Cornelia Noordam
Gerard & Alide Reesink
Helma Rem
Jan & Imma Slot
Maarten & Ge Te Hennepe
Engbert & Ietje Ubels
Tom & Esther van Aurich
Aaltje van Bergen
Rene & Lydia van den Berg
Feikje van der Haak
Lolke & Marry van der Veen
Jaap & Jelly van der Wilden
Cornelis & Jacoba van der Ziel
Cornelius & Rommy van Harten
Anton & Margreeth van Iperen
Jacobus & Jacqueline van Kleef
Aaltje (Alison) Venema
Gerardus & Margot Vinkesteyn
Philippus & Sieda Wester
Marinus & Elizabeth Wiering

Norway Division

Agot Bergli
Sigmund & Ingjerd Evensen
Kjell-arne & Elsie Haldorsen
Kari Kiserud
Ole B. Jorm Kristensen
Anne Kari Sorknes
Kare Stromme
Dag & Asa Wendel
John Richard & Inger-lise Wroughton

New Zealand Division

Fay Barker
Kristen Barnes
Joan Blaymires
Ray & Merle Brubaker
Janet Cathie
Ross & Kathleen Caughley
Vida Chenoweth
Geoffrey & Bonnie Copland
Lorraine Dougan
Robert & Deborah Early
David & Christine Foris
Edward & Christine Furby
Leo & Ingrid Geerlings
Margaret Gordon
Nancy Gray
Ngaire Hughes
Glennis Hunt
Graham & Margaret James
Harold & Pamela Jourdain
Roger & Beverley Kennedy
Jean Kirton
Janet Lee
Judith Leslie
Kenneth & Erica Mathews
Samuel & Nancy McBride
Roger & Muriel McKee
Ross & Mary McKerras
Pamela Memory
Peggy Memory
Shirley Mills
Kevin & Wendy Nicholls
Desmond & Jennifer Oatridge
Kemp & Anne Pallesen
Robert & Deborah Petterson
Dorothy Price
David Price
Rosalie Rentz
Veda Rigden
Jerry & Janet Robinson
David & Susan Ross
Barrie & Gay Stephens
Gary & Glenys Sweetman
Bruce & Carol Symons

Peru Division

Jose & Margaret Estrella
Conrad & Irma Phelps
Luisa Pinto
Ezequiel & Elena Romero

Philippines Division

Kermit & Raquel Titrud

South Africa Division

David & Margaret Abernethy
Leonard & Gillian Allwright
Timothy & Audrey Anstice
Carol Briel
Charlotte De Kock
Keith & Wilma Forster
Stanley & Cherry Graumann
Frans & Iris Haenen
Charles & Patricia Laird
Lynnette Stander
Yvonne Stofberg
Nicholas & Lynnette Swanepoel
Jan Van Wyk
Anton Vermaak

Sweden Division

Douglas & Gunnel Anderson
Gunilla Andersson
Anne-marie Andreasson
Soren & Britten Arsjo
Helene Boethius
Sune & Britt Ceder
Urs & Gerd Ernst
Bo & Margareta Hansson
Stellan & G Eivor Lindrud
Harold & Irene Ohlsson
Roland & Barbro Silen
Alfred & Irene Staiger
Gunborg Sunbring
Anders & Joyce Thelin
Kari & Susanne Valkama
Gunnar Wrang

Singapore Division

Sook Lai Lim

Switzerland Division

Frieda Berger
Dora Bieri
Margrit Bolli
Regula Bolli
Katharina Brueckner
Marlis Buehler
Ulrich & Ursula Bukies
Martin Engeler
Urs & Gerd Ernst
Timothy & Hanna Feia
Justin & Margrit Frempong
Marcel & Erika Gasser
Hanni Gassmann
Verena Geiger
Christine Gerber
Elisabeth Gfeller
Martha Giger
Erwin & Luise Gull
Hanna Gyger
E. Austin & Margrit Hale
Beat & Irma Haller
Anna Hari
Robert & Sylvia Hedinger
Claude & Christiane Heiniger
Verena Hofer
Margrit Hotz
Ruth Huerlimann
Hans-peter & Elisabeth Jufer
Anna Kohler
Jakob & Susanne Krebs
Martin & Dorothee Kruesi
Hanna Kuhn
Margrit Kuratli
Ernst Laderach
Stefan Lamprecht
Fritz & Anneke Lauffenburger
Ruth Lienhard
John & Jane Maire
Paul & Ingeborg Meier
Markus & Beatrice Meili
Anton & Heidi Mettler
Franziska Moser
Daniel & Madeleine Mosimann
Ruth Mueller
Jacques & Marie-claire Nicole
Urs Niggli
Esther Petermann
Heidi Pfeifer
Elisabeth Preisig
Irmgard Ruegg
Willi & Verena Schaub
Johanna Schmid
Hans & Esther Staehli
Martin Steib
Esther Strahm
Hanni Suter
Irma Tallowitz
Peter & Madeleine Thalmann
Alfred & Joy Tobler
Maya Weber
Urs & Johanna Wegmann
Magdalena Wichser
Fritz & Elisabeth Wunderli
Elizabeth Wyss
David & Erika Zimmermann

United States Division

Edna Aaron
Elinor Abbot
Edward & Neva Abbott
Arne & Joyce Abrahamson
Stanley Abrahamson
Stephen Abrahamson
Elizabeth Acton
Karen Adams
Patsy Adams
Donald & Clara Adams
Earl & Elizabeth Adams
Michael Adams
Alfred & Anna Jo Adan
Alfred & Donna Adan
Wayne & Marilyn Aeschliman
Ulys & Verna Aeschliman
Daniel & Margaret Agee
Walter & Marilyn Agee
Arlene Agnew
James & Nancy Agnor
Gene & Bobby Ahrens
Reva Akens
Paula Akerson
James & Susan Akovenko
John Albrecht
James & Barbara Albright
Richard & Roslyn Albright
David & Patrice Aldrich
Ruth Alexander
Victor & Virginia Alfsen
Neftali Alicea
Barbara Allen
Gay Allen
Gerald & Janice Allen
John & Joann Allen
Lawrence & Janet Allen
Roy & Lois Allen
Joe & Karen Allison
John & Jean Alsop
Kenneth & Lucile Altig
Barbara Alvarez
Arthur & Zola Alyea
John & Annette Amdahl
George & Penny Anast
William & Miriam Anders
Dorothy Andersen
Cathy Anderson
Elizabeth Anderson
Judith Lynn Anderson
Loretta Anderson
Martha Anderson
Alfred & Patsy Anderson
Clifford & Judith Anderson
John & Joy Anderson
Lambert & Doris Anderson
Michael & Thera Anderson
Neil & Carol Anderson
Ronald & Janice Anderson
Stephen & Juliette Anderson
James & Judith Andrew
Carolynn Andrews
Henrietta Andrews
Edward & Neva Andrews
Julia Andrus
Erik & Elin Andvik
John & Harriette Annis
Stuart Anthony
Evan & Nancy Antworth
Don & Sue Apgar
Douglas & Marianne Arcangeli
Jonathan & Barbara Arensen
Penny Armour
Malcolm Armour
Philip & Kathleen Armstrong
Richard & Judith Aschenberg
Herman & Elizabeth Aschmann
Richard & Heidi Aschmann
Elmer & Ruth Ash
Carolyn Ashby
Seymour & Lois Ashley
William & Ruth Atherton
Lynn & Loren Attwood
Jeanne Austin
Hayden & Frances Austin
Thomas & Kristen Avery
Michael & Faith Axman
Nancy Babe
Wendy Bachman
Glen & Shirley Bacon
Robert Bacon
Phillip & Mary Baer
Phillip & Sarah Baer
Pamela Bailey
John & Shelley Bailey
Kenneth & Leanne Bailey
Susan Baird
Nathan & Judith Baker
Lee & Arlene Ballard
Lester & Marjorie Bancroft
Nancy Bandiera
Kathleen Banker
John & Betty Banker
James & Betty Baptista
Stephen & Betsy Barber
Milton & Muriel Barker
Ronald & Martha Barkey
James & Caroline Barkley
E Keith Barkman
Edward & Jean Barkman
Eldon & Sandra Barkman
Rodolfo Barlaan
Myra Barnard
Janet Barnes
Robert & Dawn Barnes
Don & Sharon Barr
Pamela Barre
Rodrigo & Carol Barrera
John & Rebecca Barrett
Eric & Susan Bartels
Robert & Peggy Bartels
Dixon & Doralice Barthel
Doris Bartholomew
Ruth Bartholomew
Paul & Grace Bartholomew
Priscilla Bartram
Richard & Carla Bartsch
Burton & Marvel Bascom
Harry & Alma Bascom
Michael & Margaret Bashkov
Louise Bass
Janet Bateman
Norma Bates
Amy Bauernschmidt
Loren & Pamela Baughman
Willis & Phyllis Baughman
Neil Baumgartner
Edgar & Elenore Beach
Doris Beachy
Margaret Bean
Mark & Patti Bean
Sharon Beasley
David & Nancy Beasley
Harold & Ellen Beaty
Keith & Mary Beavon
Alice Beebe
Elaine Beekman
Thomas & Mary Beekman
Ricky & Roberta Bekius
Dan & Frances Bell
Gary & Jane Bell
Wesley & Jean Bell
Richard & Patricia Beller
Madelyn Beltz
Daryl & Leshia Beltz
Taik & Kaye Benaissa
Paul & Cheryl Bendele
Philip & Dorcas Benner
Verland & Lucille Benning
Willard & Ruth Benning
Bruce & Janice Benson
Joseph & Mary Benton
Marie Berg
Kathleen Bergman
Richard & Nancy Bergman
Truman (Ted) & Gwendolyn Bergman
Jim & Loanna Bergthold
Donald & Wilma Bernd
Jacqueline Bernhardt
Vina Berry
La Vera Betts
Fred & Leila Bevensee
Robert & Nancy Beversdorf
John & Anita Bickford
Janice Biegel
Gregory & Kathleen Bierbaum
Deborah Binaghi
Ronald & Kathleen Binder
Nancy Bishop
Ruth Bishop
Nita Bjorke
Doris Bjorkman
Nancy Black
Andrew & Cheryl Black
Barbara Blackburn
Betty Blair
Franklin Blair
Lee & Mamie Blaisdell
Mary Blake
Joseph & Geraldine Blakeslee
Richard & Peggy Blauser
Marcia Bleeker
Stephen & Kim Blewett
Owen Blickensderfer
Richard & Faith Blight
Evangeline Blood
David & Doris Blood
Turner & Bethel Blount
Rhonda Boaz
Bruce & Claire Bodenstein
Bruce & Claire Bodenstein,
Leonard & May Boehm
David Bohm
Rosemary Bolton
Alexander & Pamela Bolyanatz
Linda Bonasera
Carol Bondurant
Marjorie Bondurant
Patricia Bonnell
Daniel Bonnell
Willem & Carolyn Bontkes
Robert & Debra Boogaard
David & Rebecca Boos
Joseph & Lillian Boot
Fred & Grace Borden
Marlyette (Bub) & Roberta Borman
Carol Borreson
David & Janice Bothwell
Alfred & Susan Boush
Michael & Alanna Boutin
Ruth Bower
Walter & Joy Bowles
Hope Bowling
Mary Bowling
Barbara Bowman
Howard & Shirley Bowman
Phillip & Patrea Bowser
Douglas & Marilyn Boyd
John & Colleen Boyd
Perry & Sandi Bradford
Virginia Bradley
Henry & Barbara Bradley
William & Diana Bradshaw
Sherri-Lynn Brainard
Tracy Brander
Beverly Brandrup
Thomas & Judith Branks
James Brase
John & Alice Brawand
Kay Brekke
Ross & Brenda Brennan
Robert & Felicia Brichoux
Loraine Bridgeman
Ricky & Denice Bridgman
Patricia Brien
David & Joyce Briley
Lisa Brinker
Leslie & Sara Brinkerhoff
Richard & Carol Brinneman
Vernon & Carolyn Broadfield
Bonnie Brobston
Joseph & Jill Brock
Cindy Brockman
Earl & Gertrude Brockway
Phyllis Broekema
Richard & Karen Bronson
Pauline Brood
David & Gwendolyn Brooks
Henry & Lorraine Brooks
Karen Brown
Darrell & Lenore Brown
Ivan Brown
Robert Brown
William & Jane Brown
Daniel & Lucia Brubaker
Ray & Merle Brubaker
Leslie & Kathleen Bruce
Gerald & Carmen Brumley
George & Linda Bruneau
Frederick & Dorothy Bruner
Herbert & Myrtle Brussow
Samuel & Pamela Bryant
Marjorie Buck
Andrew & Rhonda Buckingham
Robert & Salme Bugenhagen
Ernest Buller
Samuel & Joanne Bullers
James & Theresa Bunge
Curtis & Estelle Bunney
Stephen & Kathy Burden
Scott Burford
Jonathan & Nancy Burmeister
Carol Burnap
Eugene & Martha Burnham
Donald & Nadine Burns
Julia Burpee
Phyllis Burpee
Donald & Edith Burquest
David & Lois Burris
James & Betty Burroughs
Bryan & Shirley Burtch
Alan & Karen Buseman
Robert & Marilyn Busenitz
John & Elsie Bush
Daryl & Marlene Bussert
Randall & Margret Buth
Inez Butler
Nancy Butler
Daniel & Barbara Butler
Danny & Mary Butler
James & Judy Butler
Ella Button
Carol Cable
Michael Cahill
Gary & Shirley Caldwell
Janet Camburn
Elizabeth Camp
Helen Campbell
Verna Campbell
Carl & Jo-Ann Campbell
Philip & Denise Campbell
Robert & Barbara Campbell
Don & Myrle Canonge
David & Linda Captain
Robert Care
Timothy & Louise Carey
Richard & Fran Carl
James & Monica Carlin
Ruth Carlson
Paul & Ellen Carlson
Paul & Lydia Carlson
Peter & Carmosina Carlson
Robert & Joyce Carlson
Terry & Julie Carlson
G Morris & Harriett Carney
Jane Carns
John & Ruth Carr
Frederick Carress
Brian & Victoria Carroll
Melvin & Billie Carson
James & Deborah Cartwright
Eugene & Betty Casad
Roderic & Ellen Casali
Daniel & Dorothy Case
Larry & Ann Cates
Marilyn Cathcart
Marvin & Twyla Catlett
Dorothea Cavett
Einar & Joan Cederholm
Jean Chaffee
Karen Chalfant
John & Marie Champ
Julia Chandler
Robert & Carol Chaney
Robert & Elaine Chappell
Kristen Chapple
Carol Chase
Donald & (Gretchen) Cheney
Robert & Dixie Cherry
Thomas & Joanne Chesebro
William Chesley
Ann Choate
Daniel & Ruth Choisser
John & Leslie Christian
Stanley Christy
Clarence & Katherine Church
Glenford & Linda Claassen
Carolyn Clapper
Burton & Glenna Clark
Gilbert & Norma Clark
Lawrence & Nancy Clark
Richard & Nadine Clark
Stephen & Dawn Clark
Kathleen Clarke
Benjamin & Diane Clary
William & Beverly Claypool
Joycelyn Clevenger
John & Deborah Clifton
William & Mary Close
Paul & Grace Closius
Elyce Cobb
Maxwell & Vurnell Cobbey
Fain (Pat) & Joanne Cochran
Dennis & Nancy Cochrane
James & Dorritee Cockerill
Maurice & Betty Cogar
Patrick & Nancy Cohen
Michael & Sandra Colburn
Fred Colby
Howard & Elizabeth Collard
Millard & Virginia Collins
Wesley & Nancy Collins
Edwin & Debra Condra
Kimberly Congdon
Mattie-Joy Congdon
Lyle & Carol Ann Connet
Robert & Jo Ann Conrad
Lynn & Jeannette Conver
Dorothy Cook
Marjorie Cook
George & Ok-Tan Cook
Henry & Elsie Cook
David & Heidi Coombs
Beatrice Cooper
Janice Cooper
Sherilyn Cooper
Verla Cooper
James & Nancy Cooper
Kenneth Cooper
Russell & Mary Cooper
Todd & Sharon Cooper
Mildred Copeland
O Geoffrey & Bonnie Copland
David Corrigan
Carole Cothran
Ken Cottrell
James & Chelle Courter
Allan & Kathryn Courtright
Ruth Cowan
George & Florence Cowan
David Coward
Diane Cowie
Samuel Cowles
Thomas & Linda Cox
Jean Crabtree
David & Joan Cram
Theodore & Terry Crandall
Clarice Crawford
Irvin & Mary Crawford
Lynn & Ruth Crawford
Robert & Dallas Creson
Gloria Cristelli
William & Ellen Cristobal
Linda Criswell
Robert & Joan Critchfield
Mark Crocker
Robert & Marcia Croese
Marjorie Crofts
Paul & Cynthia Crosbie
Oliver & Angie Crosby
Charissa Crossley
Marjorie Crouch
Thomas & Janet Crowell
Bryan Croxton
Otis Crutchfield
Elizabeth Cudney
Helen Cutler
Jeffrey & Lucille D'Jernes
Glenda Dabbs
James & Carole Daggett
Gail & Joanne Dailey
Walter & Diane Dalessio
John & Margaret Daly
Howard & Phyllis Daniel
Russell & Stella Daniels
Betty Darden
Christopher & Janell Darling
Casper & Patricia Darr
James & Linda Daubenmier
Deana Davidson
Alice Davis
Marjorie Davis
Patricia Davis
Ruth Davis
Daniel & Barbara Davis
Donald & Launa Davis
Irvine & Florence Davis
Kenneth & Donnajean Davis
Reid & Janice Davis
Beverly Dawson
Francis (Bus) & Jean Dawson
Dwight Day
Robert & Clazina de Craene
Sheryl De Lozier
Steven De Rose
Philip & Janet Deal
Saralee Debley
James & Margaret Decker
William & Cynthia Decker
John & Mary Jane Dedrick
Easter Dehaan
Ellis & Katherine Deibler
Lloyd & Roberta Deister
Debra Deitke
Walter & Beverlee Del Aguila
Valerie Delombard
Pierre & (Meg) DeMers
Kathleen Demey
J Douglas & Susan Demick
Douglas & Sue Deming
Thomas & Tonya Denney
Ronald & Margaret Dennis
David & E Jane Denyer
Leo & Valorie Depaul
George & Dorothy DeVoucalla
James & Sandra DeVries
Gino DiBartolomeo
Fredric & Wylene Dickerman
John & Joan Dickey
Annette Dickson
Lon & Louise Diehl
Paul & Deborah Diehl
Darla Dietsch
Michael & Janeen Dillow
Robert & Marjorie Dix
Gary & Deborah Doan
Rose Dobson
Lawrence & Lois Dodds
Jerome & Pauline Dodson
Frank & Denise Doejaaren
Jean Donaldson
E & Lois Donmoyer
Barbara Doolan
Robert & Kathie Dooley
Clifford & Grace Dorn
Phyllis Doty
Stephen Doty
Granville & Florence Dougherty
Gillis & Gene Douglass
Lynn Downey
Michael & Rebecca Downey
Samuel Downing
Daniel & Rosemarie Doyle
Marjorie Draper
Gordon & Cynthia Druvenga
Raymond & Marjorie Dubert
Carl & Lauretta Dubois
Jonathan & Cora Duerksen
Paul & Norma Duffey
Dale & Linda Duhe'
Nancy Duncan
David Duncan
David & Geraldine Duncan

Gordon & Diane Duncan
Howard & Cynthia Duncan
Thomas Duncan
Tommy & Tina Dunckel
Patricia Dunn
Phyllis Dunn
Janice Durette
Ronald & Ruth Durie
Paul & Peggy Dvorak
Wayne & Sally Dye
Tenesa Dyer
Carolyn Dyk
Egbert & Hattie Dyk
Steven & Debra Dyk
Dennis & Susan Dyvig
Francis Eachus
Donald & Janet Eagan
Lucille Eakin
Robert & Katherine Earl
Lester & Natalie Earp
Guy & Jeanne East
Elizabeth Eastman
Gary & Mary Eastty
Mike & Heather Eastwood
Cynthia Eaton
Roy & Julia Eberhardt
Stephen & Pamela Echerd
William & Connie Eckerle
Paul & Ann Eckert
William & Maxine Eddy
Susan Edgar
Ronald & Lois Edilson
Patrick & Melenda Edmiston
Phillip Edmiston
Debra Edwards
Elizabeth Edwards
Michael Edwards
George & Elsie Ehara
Ronald & Mae Ehrenberg
Ralph & Mary Eichenberger
William & Harriett Eichmeyer
Sonya Eidsvoog
Bobbye Eiland
Elizabeth Ekdahl
Jonathan & Margaret Ekstrom
Gerald & Evelyn Elder
James & Karen Eliason
Richard & Betty Elkins
Jo-Lynn Eller
Karen Ellertson
Raymond & Helen Elliott
Craig Ellis
James Ellis
George & Kathryn Ellison
Richard Ellison
Benjamin & Adelle Elson
Virginia Embrey
Rachel Engel
Ralph & Mary Engel
Edith Eno
James & Beverly Entz
Darrel & Cheryl Eppler
Alice Erath
Aprile Erbe
Paul & Nanci Erkert
Beverly Ernst
Ross & Ellen Errington
Patsy Eskew
Douglas & Judith Estabrook
Jose & Margaret Estrella
Marlene Etter
Donna Evans
Donald & Gail Evans
Daniel & Keren Everett
Edmund & Grace Fabian
Donna Fahnestock
David & Gloria Farah
Alan & Delores Farlin
Robin & Marva Farnsworth
James & Cynthia Farr
Kevin & Deanna Farrell
Edwin & Kathryn Farris
Gerhard & Ruby Fast
Norma Faust
Edward Fears
Timothy & Deanna Feaver
Eleanor Feerst
Timothy & Hanna Feia
Dorothy Feil
Thomas & Becky Feldpausch
Michael & Susan Felz
Michael & Deborah Fenley
Judith Ferguson
Gerald & Susan Ferguson
William & Marcia Ferguson
William & Cheryl Anne Fetrow
Harriet Fields
Philip & Gale Fields
Marianne Finkbeiner
Daniel & Kay Finley
James & Diane Finn
Lynne Fiore
Jay & Dorothy Fippinger
Irwin & Jacqueline Firchow
Karoline Fisher
Wayne & Joanne Fitch
Frank & Carol Fitzgerald
Rachel Flaming
Susan Flatt
Eric Fleischman
Lillian Fleischmann
Caroline Fleming
Ilah Fleming
Lawrence Fleming
George & Alda Fletcher
Marlene Flier
Rick & Melanie Floyd
Cheryl Fluckiger
David & Sherryl Foord
Ilene Foote
Walter & Jacquelyn Ford
Kathleen Forfia
Carl & Kathleen Forney
Joanne Forsberg
Vivian Forsberg
Jannette Forster
David & Gretchen Fortune
Philip & Janice Foster
Kim & Carolyn Fowler
David & Carol Fox
Edmund Fox
Kerry & Jean Foxworth
Joseph & Helen France
David & Lynn Frank
Paul & Margaret Frank
Vernon & Newton Frank
Vernon & Susan Frank
Karl & Joice Franklin
Kirk & Christine Franklin
Chester & Marjorie Frantz
Donald & Patricia Frantz
Michael & Anne Franusich
Roy & Cheryl Fraunhofer
James & Cora Frederick
Joni Fredrickson
Robert French
Allen & Marlene Freudenburg
Alexander & Viola Frew
Paul & Dorothy Freyberg
Timothy & Barbara Friberg
Donald & Virginia Frisbee
Kaye Froehlich
Charles & Jeanne Frost
Nancy Fry
Christopher & Pauli Fry
Leroy & Ruth Frye
Earl & Eugenia Fuller
Eugene & Carol Fuller
David & Beth Fulmer
James Fultz
Leo & Doris Funk
Herbert & Grace Fuqua
Ronald Fuqua
Ronnie & Dianna Gainer
Michael & Joy Gallagher
Andrew & Sherry Gallman
Gregory & Carolyn Gammon
Kenneth & Virginia Gammon
Janet Garcia
Donna Gardiner
Mary Gardner
George & Joan Gardner
Gerald & Nancy Gardner
Royall & Barbara Gardner
Richard & Laura Gardner
William & Lori Gardner
Roger & Susan Garland
Martha Garrard
Leonard & Wanda Garreans
Dennis & Patricia Garretson
Kenneth & Victoria Garrison
Eileen Gasaway
Rex & Judy Gasteiger
Donald & Julie Gates
Coral Gaudet
John & Elaine Gaulden
Jo Ann Gault
Chelsea Gaunt
Derek & Debra Gavette
Linda Gawthorne
Laura Gay
Winnie Gentry
Janet George
James & Susan George
Paul & Wanda George
Florence Gerdel
Phyllis Gerhardt
Glenn & Marcia Gero
Wilfred & Lana Gesch
Cheryl Gibbons
Terrance & Lynn Gibbs
William & Laurel Gibbs
Lorna Gibson
Glenn & Betty Gibson
John & Beth Gibson
Stanley & Patricia Gibson
Timothy Gier
Richard & Ruth Gieser
Rudolf & Jennifer Giezendanner
Homer & Rae Gifford
Charles & Judith Giles
Leoma Gilley
Harold & Florence Gilman
Roger & Kathleen Gilstrap
Rosemary Gingery
Jeffrey & Catherine Girard
Joseph & Mildred Girard
Peter & Laura Gittlen
C David & Barbara Glaser
David & Kathleen Glasgow
Lois Glass
Roy & Edith Gleason
Suellyn Glidden
Naomi Glock
Ronald & Ruth Gluck
Jean Goddard
Susan Goddard
Thomas & Beth Godfrey
Marie Goehner
Robert & Joyce Goerz
Merrilee Goins
Theodore & Patricia Goller
Rolando & Margaret Gonzalez
Elaine Good
Harold & Caryle Good
Harold & I Juanita Goodall
David & Kathy Goodson
Ellen Gordon
Sonia Gordon
Kent & Sandra Gordon
Raymond & Lillian Gordon
Virgil & Gladys Gottfried
Philip & Ann Graber
Ronald & Wilma Grable
Charlotte Graham
Albert & Sue Graham
Glenn Graham
Mcvey & Doris Graham
Stephen & Katrina Graham
Tim & Susan Graham
Frances Gralow
Christian & Louise Grandouiller
Barbara Grant
Jay & Beth Grant
Melvin & Eleanor Grant
Gilles & Gloria Gravelle
Cheryl Green
Harold & Diana Green
Mary Greene
Clifford & Melba Greene
Kenneth & Judith Greenlee
Charles Greenlund
Ken & Marilyn Gregerson
Perry Greninger
Margie Griffin
Robert & Louise Griffin
Paul & Claudia Griffith
Charles & Barbara Grimes
Joseph & Barbara Grimes
Vola Griste
Joel & Cindy Groening
Randall Groff
Frederick & Esther Gross
Philip & Barbara Grossman
Jeanne Grover
Steven & Jerri Gunderson
Judith Gunn
Robert & Mary Gunn
Sherman & Bernadette Guyer
Linda Haabak
Sharon Haag
Jean Hadley
Lawrence & Nancy Hagberg
Jean Haggar
Patricia Hakanson
Paul & Debra Haken
E. Austin & Margrit Hale
Michael & Sharon Hale
William & Doris Hall
Victor & Helena Halterman
Martha Ham
Gerald & Eunice Hamill
Janet Hammer
Louis & Carol Hammock
Grace Hammond
Roberta Hampton
William & Paula Hanna
Bruce & Beth Hanson
Henry & Ethel Hanssen
Richard & Mary Harbin
Janet Hardie
Barbara Hardin
David & Susanne Hargrave
Harry & Geri Harm
Richard & Brenda Harman
Bryan & Joan Harmelink
John & Mollie Harmon
Phillip & Judith Harms
Michael & Beverley Harrar
Deborah Harrell
Jerry & Betty Harrell
Suzanne Harris
Susan Harris
Kenneth & Constance Harris
Larry & Mary Harris
Robert Harris
Roy & Kathy Harris
Jayne Harrison
Carl & Carole Harrison
Daniel & Shelby Harrison
Robert & Becky Harrison
Gretchen Harro
George & Helen Hart
Rhonda Hartell
David & Janet Harthan
Elsie Hartog
Darlene Hartshorn
Patricia Hartung
Donald & Marlene Hartzell
Dwight & Margaret Hartzler
Michael & Carole Harvey
Peggy Harvie
David & Jean Hastings
Patterson Hastings
Freeman & Corine Hatch
Michael & Karen Hatfield
Ralph & Lorraine Haupers
Mike Hause
Frank Hawfield
Cecil & June Hawkins
Nancy Haynes
Clara Hazelwood
Paul & Edna Headland
Thomas & Janet Headland
Mary Heard
Daniel & Teresa Heath
Terry & Cheryl Heffield
Arlo & Viola Heinrichs
John Heins
Carol Heinze
Allene Heitzman
Donald & Martha Hekman
Greg Henderson
John & Linda Henderson
Gail Hendrickson
David & Marilyn Henne
Lee & Lynneford Henriksen
Joan Henry
David & Marilyn Henry
Grace Hensarling
Mark & Carol Hepner
Alexander Herd
Rick Herr
Julie Herron
Henry & M Ruth Hershberger
Lester & Millicent Hershey
Russell & Lynda Hersman
Darrell & Carol Hertz
Dorothy Herzog
Harwood & Pat Hess
Victor & Valerie Hess
Don & Lois Hesse
Alice Hester
Dolores Hetteen
Leslie & Katharine Heyward
Calvin & Cornelia Hibbard
Keith & Melody Hibbard
Sharon Hicks
Michael & Patricia Highland
Henry & Barbara Hildebrandt
Faith Hill
Pamela Hill
Ralph & Harriet Hill
Richard & Roseann Hill
George & Valerie Hillman
Kenneth & Martha Hilton
Ardella Himbert
Mary Hinson
Daniel & Diane Hintz
Charles & Emilie Hipp
George & Valerie Hires
Kent & Suzanne Hirschelman
Linda Hitchcock
Stanley & Alice Hixson
Barbara Hoch
Charles & Marie Hoch
Ruth Hockett
David & Edith Hockett
Aaron & Marlene Hoffman
Ralph Hofstetter
Harold & Connie Hogan
Richard & Elma Lou Hohulin
Paul & Susan Hoiland
Arthur & Susan Holden
Bruce & Barbara Hollenbach
Kenneth & Judith Hollingsworth
Thomas & Mary Holman
Harold & Rachel Holmberg
John & Esther Holmbo
James & Janice Holsclaw
Dorothy Holsinger
Francis & Frances Holston
Andreas & Anna Holzhausen
Searle & Hilda Hoogshagen
Connie Hoover
Mary Hopkins
Bradley & Elizabeth Hopkins
Robert & Dorothy Hoppe
Mary Hopple
Elizabeth Horn
Herbert & Tamara Horn
Donald & Jane Horneman
Walter & Dorothy Horning
Edward & Charlotte Horton
Daniel Horwitz
Brenda Hostetler
John & Ann Hostetler
Roman & Carolyn Hostetler
Philip & Gwen Hostetter
Joyce Hotz
Charlotte Houck
Alan & Susan Houk
Paul Howard
Lillian Howland
Wayne & Marsha Howlett
Robert & Carol Hubbs
Kenneth & Linda Hubel
Kenneth & Gloria Huber
Randall Huber
Jack & Pamilla Huddle
Edna Hudson
Richard & Deborah Hudson
Wayne & Alice Huff
David & Linda Huffman
Susan Hugghins
Linda Hughes
Richard & Edith Hugoniot
Ronald & Roberta Huisman
Betty Huizenga
James & Marcia Hulings
Kimberly Humphrey
Marian Hungerford
Trudi Hunt
Leigh & Sharon Hunt
Georgia Hunter
Conrad & Phyllis Hurd
Fred & E Elaine Hurd
Ronald Hurst
Stewart & Jean Hussey
Edwin & Martha Hutcheson
John & Gail Hutchinson
Don & Sharon Hutchisson
Thomas & Ramey Hutson
George & Mary Huttar
Martin & Sharon Huyett
Elijah Hyde
Marvin & Joyce Hyde
Robert & Gene Hyland
David & Barbara Hynum
Donald & Joy Iden
David & Patsy Immel
Richard & Carolyn Inlow
Barbara Inman
George & Jeanne Insley
Marlin & Mariann Iszler
Catherine Jackson
Dorothy Jackson
Ellen Jackson
Frances Jackson
Arthur & Dorothy Jackson
Kenneth & Brenda Jackson
Robert & Anne Jackson
William & Evangelyn Jackson
Kenneth & Elaine Jacobs
Paul & Bonnie Jacobson
Marc & Suzanne Jacobson
Debra Jaekley
Else Jagst
Martha Jakway
Dorothy James
Theodore & Patricia James
Allan & Carole Jamieson
William & Norma Jancewicz
Richard & Gladys Janssen
John & Anna Jantzen
Dwight & Rena Jarboe
Kenneth & Elizabeth Jatko
Kathleen Jefferson
Charles & Sue Jenkins
David & Donna Jenkins
Rister & Esther Jenkins
Roger & Carolyn Jenkins
Wanda Jennings
Vickie Jensen
Allen & Cheryl Jensen
Donald & Margaret Jensen
Harry & Helen Jensen
Fred & Virginia Jessup
Dwight & Susan Jewett
James Johansson
Richard & Carol Johns
Sydney & Nola Johnsen
Audrey Johnson
Julia Johnson
Irene Johnson
Jeannette Johnson
Kathleen Johnson
Merieta Johnson
Tena Johnson
Donald & Helen Johnson
Fred & Martha Johnson
Gary & Barbara Johnson
Greg & Karen Johnson
James Johnson
Jonathan & Roseann Johnson
Orville & Mary Johnson
Paul & Dona Johnson
Rex Johnson
Richard & Katherine Johnson
Ron & Elizabethanne Johnson
Wayne & Neomi Johnson
Judith Johnston
Edward & Helen Johnston
John & Marjorie Johnston
Paul Johnston
Priscilla Jones
Donald & Joan Jones
Larry & Linda Jones
Larry & Marcia Jones
Mark & Peggy Jones
Ralph & Marie Jones
Theodore & Kristie Jones
Burton & Patricia Jones
Wendell & Paula Jones
Henry Jonson
Dean & Carol Jordan
James & Nancy Jordan
Norman & Muriel Jordan
Daniel & Cheryl Jore
Luther & Barbara Jueneman
Porter & Jeanne Kaetterhenry
Steven & Elizabeth Kaetterhenry
James Kaiser
James & Kiyoko Kakumasu
John & Carol Kalmbacher
Marjorie Kalstrom
Marit Kana
Allen & Bernelle Kanagy
Donald & Phyllis Kanaley
Mark & Elke Karan
Randall & Colleen Karcher
Janice Kausalik
Kevin & Nancy Kautz
Raymond & Frances Kay
Bryan & Mary Keef
Dorothy Keeley
Charlotte Keels
Jack & Carol Keels
Robert & Linda Keizer
Barbara Keller
Kathryn Keller
Charles & Sally Keller
Patricia Kelley
Michael Kelley
Franklyn & Miriam Kellogg
David & Dorothy Kelly
Richard & Grace Kelso
Stephen & Patricia Kempf
Walter Kennicutt
Susan Kenny
Carolyn Kent
Robert & Louella Kerstetter
Tim & Linda Kevern
William & Marjorie Key
Dale & Harriett Kietzman
Shirley Killosky
Eileen Kilpatrick
Rodney & Pamela Kinch
Eric & Mary Kindberg
Willard & Lee Kindberg
Gloria Kindell
Juliann King
Martha King
Elvin & Margaret King
Wayne & Julie King
Raymond & Lillian Kingsley
Diane Kinney
Thomas & Teri Kinnier
Marion Kirk
Will & Dorothea Kirkendall
Howard & Linda Klassen
Julie Klaver
Marquita Klaver
Gary & Carol Klingler
Ronald & Judith Klump
James & Deloris Klumpp
Ruby Knapp
Paul & Shirley Knapp
Harriet Kneeland
Richard & Diana Knieriemen
Judy Knowles
James & Elberta Knowlton
Robert & Edith Knox
Wendy Knudson
Virginia Knuebel
Edward & Sally Koehn
Douglas & Luann Kogler
Shirley (Til) Kohley
Laurine Kolderup
Victor & Riena Kondo
Gordon & Shirley Kooistra
Abram & Debra Koop
Linda Koopman
Carl & Sharon Kotapish
Edward & Janet Kotynski
Mark & Susan Kovach
Willis & Virginia Kramer
David & Hannah Kratzer
Greta Krawczyk
Dennis & Sharon Kready
Catherine Krekel
Roger & Regina Krenzin
John Kreutz
Martha Kreykes
Bernice Krieger
Serge & Margorie Krikorian
Paul & Chaw Nen Kroeger
Dean & Betty Kroeker
Menno & Barbara Kroeker
Paul & Kyle Kroening
Robert & Joyce Kruckeberg
Ronald & Joanne Krueger
Nathan & Dawn Kruger
Harold & Genevieve Kruzan
Kenneth & Carol Kruzan
Lawrence & Karen Kuch
Virginia Kuczun
Nathan & Anna Kugler
Albertha Kuiper
Florence Kuipers
Glenn & Elise Kull
Carrie Kulp
David & Patricia Kunselman
Robert & Linda Kvasnica
Darlene Kyle
John & Lois Kyle
Marcus & Elizabeth Kyle
David & Linda Lackey
William & Judy Lambright
Leo & Anne Lance
Peter Landerman
M Lynn Landweer
Bryan & Janet Lane
Mark & Faith Lane
Katherine Langan
Charles & Sidney Langston
Nancy Lanier
Bonnie Larrimore
Helen Larsen
Raymond & Kathryn Larsen
Robert & Marlys Larsen
Mildred Larson
Valentine Larson
Virginia Larson
David Larson
Thomas & Kathryn Laskowske
Marilyn Laszlo
Maxwell Lathrop
Edward & Dayle Lauber
Linda Lauck
Douglas & Carol Lauver
Donald & Phyllis Lawecki
Albert & Marlene Lawrence
Ilo Leach
Marlin & Sheryl Leaders
Otis & Mary Leal
Jim & Jeanne Leamer
Wilma Lee
Ernest & Lois Lee
Robert & Carolyn Lee
Charles & Kathryn Lehardy
Debra Lehman
Lonnie Lein
Robert Leithiser
Wayne & Elena Leman
Joan Lemke
Joseph & Janis Lenhert
Donald & Pamela Leonard
Bill & Penny Leonhard
C Edward & Linda Leslie
Karen Lewis
Mabel Lewis
Melvyn & Adalee Lewis
Ronald & Sandra Lewis
Millicent Liccardi
Reinhold & Marjorie Liedtke
Arthur & Kathleen Lightbody
Siok Tin Lim
Eddie & Cynthia Lind
John & Royce Lind
Orin & Sandra Linden
Donald & Jean Lindholm
John & Carrie Lindskoog
Richard Lindvall
David & Susan Linton
Robert & Susan Lipps
Robert & Shirley Litteral
Fred & Penny Livingston
Linda Lloyd
Darrol & Leola Lockhart
Eunice Loeweke
Rebecca Long
Jerold & Brenda Long
Theordore & Lillice Long
Robert & Gwen Longacre
Eugene & Betty Loos
Mary Lord
James & Hettie Loriot
Russel & Gail Loski
Pamela Love
Nancy Loveland
Richard & Aretta Loving
Ernest & Patricia Lowcock
Lois Lowers
F & Inez Lown
Richard & Marlene Luartes
John & Diana Lubeck
Ramona Lucht
Timothy & Joann Lueders
Jim & Edna Lush
Keith & Ruthann Lusk
Ruth Lusted
Nadine Lyman
Larry & Rosemary Lyman
Stuart & Adele Lyman
Thomas & Elnore Lyman
Robert & Connie Lynch
Stephen & Karen Lynip
Sara Lyon
Don & Shirley Lyon
Floyd & Mildred Lyon
Kelly & Jan Lyon
Gregory & Melinda Lyons
Wayne & Julene Maanum
John & Marjorie Mabry
Alan & Doris MacDonald
George & Georgetta MacDonald
Scott & Louise MacGregor
Frances MacNeill
Valerie Magner
Robert & Helen Mahaffey
Jacqueline Maier
Ruth Main
Cornelia Mak
Josephine Makil
Terrell Malone
Dennis & Susan Malone
Elizabeth Maloney
C & Marcia Manier
Stephen & Laraine Mann
Richard & Karis Mansen
John & Leslye Mantell
Ronald & Phyllis Manus
David & Louise Maranz
Lynell Marchese
David & Linda Marcy
Rundell & Judith Maree
Ronald Markham
Donna Marks
Stephen & Cathy Marlett
Thomas & Esther Marmor
Jack & Patricia Maroon
Alger & Gloria Marsh
James & Marjorie Marsh
Lester & Bernis Marsh
Dorothy Marshall
David Marshall
Helen Marten
Lana Martens
Michael & Martha Martens
Dale & Dorothy Martin
Timothy & Brenda Martin
William & Lenore Martin
Charles & Mary Marvin
John & Rhoda Marx
Kenneth & Alice Maryott
David & Kathlyn Mase
Elizabeth Masland
David & Mollie Mason
Denis & Diana Masson
Barbara Mast
Glen & Ellen Mast
Chester & Frances Matheson
Lonny Matsuda
Esther Matteson
Blake & Donna Matthews
Michael & Diane Matthews
Michael & Peggy Maxwell
Bernard & Nancy May
Audrey Mayer
Marvin & Marilyn Mayers
Roy & Georgia Lee Mayfield
Dorothy Maynard
Kenneth & Melissa Mayo
Jay & Leslee McAlevy
Richard & Carol McArthur
Phillip & Marilyn McBride
Samuel & Nancy McBride
James & Betty McCarty
Clive & Janet McClelland
Homer & Rauni McClure
Jane McClurkan
Frank & Kathleen McCollum
Stephen McConnel
Michael McCord
David McCormick
Joe & Beverly McCormick
Brooks & Barbara McCrorey
Kenneth & Noreen McElhanon
Judy McGinnis
Janet McGough
John & Genevieve McIntosh
Ronald & Karen McIntosh
Melody McIntyre
Judy McKee
Robert & Carol McKee
Fred & Ruth McKennon
Donald & Elaine McKinley
Norris & Carol McKinney
Paul & Janet McLarren
Linda McMillan
Stan & Margot McMillen
Debra McPherson
Robert & Mabel Meader
Frank & Charlotte Mecklenburg
Albert & Carole Meehan
Richard & Priscilla Mellen
Kathleen Menning
William & Grace Merrifield
Beatrice Messa
Randall & Debra Metzger
Ronald & Lois Metzger
James & Cathy Metzler
Leslie & Virginia Metzler
James Meyer
Ronald & Mary Michael
Michael Middleton
Helen Miehle
Daniel & Glenda Mielke
Harry & Patricia Miersma
Brenda Migliazza
Paul & Gertrude Milanowski
Ramona Millar
Cynthia Miller
Helen Miller
Jeanne Miller
Joyce Miller
Kathryn Miller
Marjorie Miller
Vera Miller
Daniel & Patricia Miller
Herley & Helen Miller
J Michael & Cheryl Miller
James & Marveine Miller
John & Carolyn Miller

Richard & Ruth Miller
Samuel & Wanda Miller
Vernon & Robin Miller
Lloyd & Ruth Milligan
Stuart & Margaret Milliken
Andrew & Audrey Minch
Daniel & Pamela Minor
Eugene & Dorothy Minor
Roy & Anne Minor
John & Billie Mishler
Frederick & Jeanne Miska
Penelope Mitchell
Billy & Sally Mitchell
Ronald & Elizabeth Moe
Barry & Bonita Moeckel
Patricia Moffett
Mary Mollhagen
Harold & Mildred Mollohan
Richard & Susan Montag
Victor & Anita Monus
David & Marsha Moody
Barbara Moore
Diane Moore
Sherilyn Moore
Bruce & Glenda Moore
Charles & Shirley Moore
Dean & Dianne Moore
Howard & Marilyn Moore
Hyatt & Anne Moore
J Henry & Rose Moore
Paul & Karisse Moore
Thomas & Aureol Moore
William & Diane Moore
Karl & Louise Moosbrugger
Marjory Moran
Irving & Glenda More
Mary Morgan
Rita Morgan
Frank & Jerelyn Morgan
John & Cathlyn Morrell
Ronald & Diane Morren
Janet Morris
Barbara Morse
Nancy Morse
Carl & Alice Mortenson
Gregory & Susan Jean Mortimer
Richard & Sue Mortimer
Mary Moser
Michael & Doris Motte
Alberthine Mount-Burke
Michael & Patricia Mower
Michael Moxness
Melanie Moy
Glenn & Glenda Moyer
James & Carolyn Mudge
Richard & Susan Mueller
Robert & Jan Mugele
Robert & Alice Muir
Paul & Mary Mullen
Loys Mundy
Scott & Jennifer Munger
Jo Munson
Anne Munz
John & Elizabeth Murane
Penny Murphy
Colin & Lynn Murphy
Robert & Gertrude Murphy
Don & Mary Murray
Thomas & Eileen Murray
James & Barbara Musgrove
Robert & Barbara Musser
David & Linda Mutchler
Marguerite Muzzey
Mark & Linda Myers
Kenneth & Cindy Najar
John & Beverly Nare
Michael & Rebecca Navratil
Dwayne & Carole Neal
Richard & Darlene Need
Stanley & Carolyn Neher
Lawrence & Jane Neiswender
David & Wendy Nellis
Donald & Jane Nellis
Neil & Jane Nellis
Ruth Nelsen
Mark Nelson
Paul & Karen Nelson

Robert & Marion Nelson
James & Susan Ness
Helen Neuenswander
Daniel & Suzanne New
Ronald & Susan Newberg
Susan Newberry
Mark & Phyllis Newell
John & Bonnie Newman
John & Idella Newman
Donald & Virginia Newsom
Dennis & Erna Newton
Gary & Theodocia Nicholas
Wayne & Arline Nicholes
David & Joan Nichols
Frank & Gail Nichols
John & Marilyn Nickel
Titus & Florence Nickel
Thomas & Kristine Nickell
Frederick & Linda Niehoff
Joyce Nies
Robert & Montana Nimmo
Richard & Susan Nivens
Kathy Niver
Dalton & Deanne Noack
Larry & Bonnie Noack
Judith Nordaas
Norman Nordell
Robert & Karen Norling
Joanne North
Charles & Robin North
Gene & Janet Nurkka
William & Marjory Nyman
David & Elizabeth Nyquist
Doyle & Betty Nystrom
John & Tamalee Nystrom
John & Bonnie Nystrom
Paul & Rebecca Nystrom
Daniel & Beverly O'Brien
Clare O'Leary
Russell & Margaret Obenchain
Mary Odmark
Vaughn Odom
James & Sandra Odor
David & Joan Ohlson
Charles & Patricia Ohrenschall
John & Joyce Oien
Gordon Oksnevad
Julie Olive
Evelyn Olsen
Kimber Olsen
Delores Olson
Clifford & Roxanne Olson
Dennis & Eleanor Olson
Donald & Anne Olson
Gary & Robbie Olson
James & Judith Olson
Michael & Donna Olson
Ronald & Frances Olson
David & Judith Oltrogge
William & Victoria Opie
Ruth Oram
Carolyn Orr
Raymond & Joyce Orwick
Carol Orwig
Ruth Ostry
Mark & Dorothy Ott
Willis & Rebecca Ott
John & Ida Ottaviano
Steven & Deborah Ottaviano
Joyce Overholt
Elvira Owen
Wanda Pace
Jerry Page
Hazel Palileo
Scott & Lynanne Palmer
Leo & Barbara Pankratz
Ronald & Doris Pappenhagen
Marinell Park
James & Joyce Park
Carolynn Parker
Henry & Linda Parker
Kirk & Carla Parker
Richard & Harriet Parker
Stephen Parker
Roger Parks
James & Judith Parlier
Carole Passerello
Helen Passwater

Keith & Frankie Patman
Sarah Patterson
James & Mary Patterson
Donald & Judy Patton
Jill Paullus
Debbie Paulsen
David & Judith Payne
Roy & Dorothy Payne
Thomas & Doris Payne
George & Wendy Payton
Joseph & Christina Pearo
Patrick & Sammee Pearson
Randall & Shirley Pearson
William & Mallory Pearson
Patricia Peck
Charles Peck
Lloyd & Nancy Peckham
Lois Pederson
Catherine Peeke
Alan & Patricia Pence
Jan Pepmeier
Charlene Persons
David & Jan Persons
Gary & Diane Persons
Willem & Marcia Pet
Gary Peterson
Lee Peterson
Mary Peterson
Mary Peterson
Doyle Peterson
Eric & Carol Peterson
Neal & Jane Peterson
Robert & Sylvia Peterson
Timothy & Sharon Peterson
Wayne & Marcia Phaneuf
Conrad & Irma Phelps
Martha Philips
Don & Sheila Piccone
Wilbur & Ida Pickering
Velma Pickett
Kent & Michelle Piepgrass
Wendell & Iris Piepgrass
Judson & Caroline Pierson
Eunice Pike
Kenneth & Evelyn Pike
Merrill & Winifred Piper
Michael Piper
Donald & Mary Pitman
Richard & Catherine Pittman
Robert & Linda Pittman
Arie Poldervaart
Andrew & Frances Popovich
Martin & Edna Lee Popp
Doris Porter
Glenn & Lola Porter
Rayburn Posey
Ursula Post
Carole Posthuma
Linda Potter
Todd & Karla Poulter
Daniel Povolny
Patricia Powell
Gerald & Sylvia Powell
William & Elayne Powell
Paul & Esther Powlison
Terry & Elizabeth Prange
David Presson
David & Leah Preston
Kenneth & Joyce Prettol
Anita Price
Lynne Price
Ruth Ann Price
Doyt & Irene Price
Norman & Barbara Price
Perry & Anne Priest
Willard & Marsha Pritchard
Gilbert & Marian Prost
Lenardo & Sandra Pugyao
Gregory Purnell
Norman & Patricia Purvis
Stephen & Janice Quakenbush
Philip & Rebecca Quick
Elsa Raab
Randolph & Mary Radney
Thomas & Margery Rafetto
William & Janet Rainey
James & Carole Rainsberger
James & Carole Rainsburger

Boris & Elizabeth Ramirez
David & Nancy Ramsdale
John & Shevawn Ramsey
Sharon Rand
Jeannette Ransom
Dan & Virginia Rath
Jonathan & Kathleen Rathjen
Rebecca Rawson
Chesley & Ruth Ray
Michael & Sandra Ray
Margaret Redyke
Ricky & Sharon Reece
Roger & Marilyn Reeck
Ralph & Judy Reed
Robert & Judith Reed
Wesley & Leeann Reed
Brian & Mary Reese
James Reese
Randall & Susan Regnier
Judith Rehburg
Richard & Judy Reid
Alice Reiling
Richard & Sandra Reimer
Wesley & Mary Reimer
Russell & Alberta Reinert
Robin Rempel
Paul & Joan Renkenberger
Calvin & Carolyn Rensch
Donald Renshaw
Tim Reser
Mary Rhea
Margaret Rhoads
Ralph & Kathleen Ricco
Alvin & Delores Rice
Therise Rich
Ernest & Margaret Rich
Rolland & Furne Rich
Nancy Richards
Ruth (Peggy) Richards
Russell & Mary Richards
Edwin & Susan Richardson
Richard & Mildred Richer
Ernest & Marjorie Richert
Audrey Richey
William & Delores Richmond
William & Joan Richter
Karen Ricketts
Eddy & Eva Riggle
Dave & Sylvia Riggs
Arthur & Lark Rilling
Andrew & Katherine Ring
David & Kathleen Rising
Ray & Doris Rising
Frank & Ethel Robbins
Larry & Camille Robbins
Wayne Robertson
Jerry & Janet Robinson
Peter Rochau
Mary Roe
Richard Roe
Larry & Lisa Roettger
William & Shirley Rogers
Pat Rohan
Nancy Roland
John & Claudia Rollo
Albert & Mary Roman
Joan Roraff
Danny & Vicky Rose
Gary & Margaret Rosensteel
Deborah Ross
Jean Rountree
S Rountree
Orland & Phyllis Rowan
Steven & Nancy Rowan
Kathy Rowell
Earl & Carol Rowell
Katherine Rowlett
Edward & Jacqueline Ruch
Robert & Diane Rucker
Edwin & Patricia Rumberger
James & Freda Rupp
Beth Rupprecht
David & Marsha Ruth
Jacob & Charlotta Ruth
Richard & Jacqueline Rutter
Ronald & Gloria Ryan
Glenn & Barbara Sage
John & Donna Sahlin

James & Shirin Sahnow
Thomas & Emily Salisbury
Thomas & Nancy Samples
Douglas & Anne Sampson
Bruce & Elizabeth Samuelson
Natalie Sand
Jana Sandberg
Mary Sanders
Arden & Joy Sanders
Timothy & Sharon Sandvig
Arlene Sanford
Mary Sargent
William & Marjorie Sasnett
Janice Saul
Letitia Saunders
Timothy & Lorraine Savage
Dean & Irma Sawdon
Dean & Lucille Saxton
Forest & Reatha Saylor
Thomas & Sylvia Sayre
Robert Scebold
Robert & Nancy Schaefer
Jared & Kathy Schanely
Leon & Elizabeth Schanely
Lawrence & Carol Schatz
Stanley & Junia Schauer
Thomas & Susan Schemper
John & Delores Scherling
Marilyn Schlenker
Perry & Virginia Schlie
Patrick & Susan Schmidt
Sandra Schneider
Robert & Lois Schneider
William & Miriam Schnittker
Joseph & Eleanor Schoenert
Alvin & Louise Schoenhals
Lyle & Helen Scholz
Thelma Schoolland
Wallace & Belva Schott
Terry & Judith Schram
Darryl & Marilyn Schreffler
Kent & Leila Schroeder
Marshall & Vanice Schultz
Audrey Schumacher
Ronald & Donna Schumacher
Julie Schwandt
Norman & Sandra Schwartz
David & Jacqueline Scorza
Claudia Scott
Eugene & Marie Scott
Thomas Scroggs
Robert & Barbara Seavey
Dennis & Janet Seever
George & Christine Semerenko
Paul & Joyce Setter
John & Elizabeth Sexton
Dorothy Shaler
John & Anna Shanks
Louis & Lisa Shanks
Allan & Barbara Shannon
Gene & Patricia Shannon
Claude & Priscilla Sharpe
Dallas & Carol Shattuck
Patricia Shaulis
David Shaver
Dwight & Gwynne Shaver
Harold & M Elizabeth Shaver
Mary Shaw
Daniel & Karen Shaw
Susan Shay
Eula Sheffler
Sally Shekleton
Robert & Dana Shelby
Howard & Deidre Shelden
Steven & Linda Sheldon
Charles Shelton
James & Joyce Shephard
Gary & Barbara Shepherd
Gilbert & Lorna Shepherd
Virginia Sheppard
Mary Sherburn
Margaret Sherburne
Grace Sherman
Betsy Sherwood
Joanne Shetler
Donna Shewmaker
Daniel & Louise Sheyda
Jana Shields

David & Marilene Shinen
Gary & Charlotte Shingledecker
Susan Shipp
Ivagene Shive
Jack & Nola Shoemaker
Hazel Shorey
Stuart Showalter
Richard & Colleen Shultz
Barbara Sidbury
Sadie Sieker
Armon & Elona Siemsen
David & Karen Sifert
Peter & Sheryl Silzer
Ruth Simmons
Gary & Linda Simons
Christopher & Anne Sims
Donald & Isabel Sinclair
William Sischo
Lois Skellenger
Harold & Gladys Skinner
Leonard & Marlene Skinner
Marianna Slocum
Priscilla Small
Joan Smith
Delores Smith
Jean Smith
Jill Smith
Margaret Smith
Mary Smith
Norma Smith
Clifford & Margery Smith
Donald & Barbara Smith
Donald & Jeanne Smith
Evan & Carol Smith
Gene & Gertrude Smith
Glenn & Linda Smith
Jonathan & Dawn Smith
Kenneth & Marilyn Smith
Larry & Nancy Smith
Paul & Dorothy Smith
Paul & Joyce Smith
Paul & Karen Smith
Ralph & Catharine Smith
Richard & Connie Smith
Terrence & Karla Smith
Thomas & Elizabeth Smoak
James & Olivia Smoot
Davis & Elaine Smoot
James & Lorraine Smotherman
Jeffrey & Josephine Smotherman
Ronald & Esther Snell
Wayne & Betty Snell
David & Ruth Snyder
Sharon Soesbe
David & Carole Spaeth
Margarethe Sparing
Craig & Patricia Spaulding
Arthur & Barbara Speck
Charles & Jane Speck
Richard & Marilyn Speece
Randall & Anna Speirs
David & Becky Spencer
Edward & Linda Spegers
Roger & Ruth Spielmann
Mary Spilman
John & Carol Spitzack
John & Karen Spitzli
Rebecca Sporhase
Hazel Spotts
Clifford & Fay Spracklin
Jacquelyn Spruill
Philip & Lorraine Staalsen
Michael & Joyce Stach
Charles & June Stacy
James Stahl
Howard & Donna Stahlman
James & Vera Stair
Glenn & Emily Stairs
William & Rochelle Staley
Tricia Stanley
Sharon Stark
John & Janie Stark
Robert & Carol Starr
Richard & Carolyn Steele
Esther Steen
Roman & Janice Stefaniw
John & Elizabeth Steketee

Kaye Stender
Bertha Stephens
Robert & Joyce Sterner
Richard & Carol Steuart
John & Eleanor Stevens
Paul Stevenson
Anne Stewart
Trudy Stewart
Donald & Shirley Stewart
Glenn & Judy Stewart
Cloyd & Ruth Stewart
Irene Stillings
Paul Stevenson
Anne Stewart
Trudy Stewart
Donald & Shirley Stewart
Glenn & Judy Stewart
Cloyd & Ruth Stewart
Irene Stillings
Timothy & Donna Stime
George & Vivie Stiteler
Judson & Beth Stocker
Joel & Nancy Stolte
Ronald & Sharon Stoltzfus
Harold & Linda Stone
Kurt & Margarete Storck
Warren & Dolores Storm
Miriam Stout
David & Gladys Strange
George & Patty Strange
Dennis & Jean Stratmeyer
Sallie Strickland
Hershel Strickland
Clayton & Beverly Strom
Clarice Strong
Charles & Janet Strong
John & Donna Stuart
Morris & Carol Stubblefield
Alfred & Dellene Stucky
Daniel & Lorraine Stucky
Galen & Bonnie Stutzman
Alvin & Shirley Suderman
Nancy Suiter
Terrence Sullivan
James Sutton
Edwin & Doris Svedberg
Gordon & Thelma Svelmoe
Dorothy Svendsen
Jeanette Swackhamer
Heather Swanson
Douglas & Janet Swanson
Stephen & Beverly Swartz
Richard & Naomi Swartzendruber
Ernest & Peggy Swartzentruber
Wesley & Harriet Swauger
Johanna Swenson
Ronald Swick
Kenneth & Joy Swift
Alger & Kathleen Syme
John & Linda Szymanski
Mark Taber
Doyle & Penelope Tallman
Linder & Mae Tanksley
Carolyn Taylor
Frank & Margaret Taylor
James & Janelle Teasdale
Stephen Teel
Philip & Susan Tees
Tamara Templin
Brian & Judith Tenny
Douglas & Carorolyn Tharp
Scott & Janet Thaxton
Wesley & Eva Thiesen
Henry & Beverly Thimell
Lisbeth Thomas
Curtis & Claudia Thomas
David & Dorothy Thomas
J & Barbara Thomas
Jerry & Elder Thomas
Ned & Kathleen Thomas
Robert & E Carolyn Thomas
Robert & Jo Ann Thomas
Linda Thompson
Nancy Thompson
Henry Thompson
Peter & Donna Thorne
James & Nancy Thrasher

Stephen & Marilyn Thrasher
Craig & Linda Throop
Robert & Ruth Thurman
Ronald & Rhonda Thwing
Cheryl Tiffany
Tessa Tilley
George & Eloise Tilt
Kermit & Raquel Titrud
Michael Titus
Beverly Todd
Ralph & Marey Todd
Terry & Patricia Lynn Todd
Lora Toedter
Donald & Norma Toland
Ralph & Marilynn Toliver
Phyllis Tolliver
Douglas Towne
Elaine Townsend
Alfred & Janice Townsend
Paul & Sharon Townsend
Francis & Donna Tozier
Hubert & Martha Tracy
Ronald & Gail Trail
Michael & Donna Trainum
Marie Trapani
Edgar Travis
Gregory Trihus
Darrel & Ada Trimble
Robert & Martha Tripp
Edwin (Tony) & Nargis Trowbridge
Mary Troyer
Lester & Madeline Troyer
Margaret Tucker
James & Alice Tucker
Alfred & Pamela Tuggy
David & Joy Tuggy
John & Sheila Tuggy
John & Lucille Tumas
Janet Turner
Blaine & Patricia Turner
Glen & Jeannie Turner
Jack & Janet Turner
Nancy Turtle
Daniel Tutton
James & Janis Tyhurst
Edward & Virginia Ubels
Matthew & Rosemary Ulrich
Faith Underhill
Lillian Underwood
David & Rebecca Underwood
Gary & Shirley Unruh
Peter & Carole Unseth
Randolph & Lisa Valentine
Haig & Paula Valenzuela
Rene & Phyllis Vallette
Donald & Gail Van Den Berg
Victor & Margaret Van Duser
Julia Van Dyken
Thomas & Terry Van Gorkom
Nancy Van Halsema
Wilhelmina Van Krieken
Trudy Van Noord
David & Donna Van Nortwick
Beth Van Ormer
Roger & Karen Van Otterloo
Stephen & Judy Van Rooy
Marian Van Sickle
Donald & Mabel Van Wynen
Robert & Katherine Van Zyl
Randy & Carolyn Vaughan
Virginia Velie
Renee Vick
Alexander & Lois Vincent
Dennis & Terry Vincent
Norman Vissering
Alan Vogel
Katherine Voigtlander
Paul & Karen Vollrath
Janie Voss
Ruth Vreeland
Joseph & Marilyn Waddington
Claire Wagner
John & Donna Wagner
Richard & Joanne Wagner
Richard & Ramona Wagner
Stanley & Diane Wagner

David & Frances Wakefield
Bonnie Walker
Janice Walker
James & Mary Walker
James & Shelley Walker
Larry & Sharon Walker
Richard & Shirley Walker
Roland & Jean Walker
Stephen & Mary Lou Walker
Robert & Mary Walker
Larry & Gloria Wall
Judith Wallace
Donald & Cynthia Wallace
John & Adreanna Waller
Ethel Wallis
Joe & Janette Walter
Stephen & Leah Walter
Charles & Janice Walton
James & Janice Walton
John & Marjorie Walton
Nathan & Carolyn Waltz
Susan Ward
Michael & Lorna Ward
Samuel & Julia Ward
Ruth Wardell
Alan & Iris Wares
Donald & Eunice Warfel
Susan Warkentin
Viola Warkentin
Joel & Marjorie Warkentin
Milton & Clara Warkentin
James & Lou Warner
Edward & Linda Warnock
Hardy Warren
Viola Waterhouse
William & Anna-Louise Waters
J Paul Watkins
Richard & Saundra Watson
David & Nancy Watters
James & Juanita Watters
John & Kathie Watters
Kenneth & Vivian Watters
Frances Weathermon
Dale & Susan Weathers
Kenneth Weathers
Mark & Esther Weathers
Deborah Weaver
Linda Weaver
Martha Weaver
Daniel & Mary Weaver
Jay & Carol Weaver
David & Diana Weber
Donald & Annabell Weber
Robert & Nancy Weber
Mervin & Carol Weberg
Darlene Weidman
Harry Weimer
James & Shirley Weimer
Robert & Donna Weimer
Jeffrey & Ann Weir
Peter & Linda Weissenburger
Betty Welch
Anita Wencker
Margaret Wendell
Thomas & Jane Werkema
Patricia Werkman
Anne West
Birdie West
Edith West
David & Virginia West
Frederic & Marilyn West
Oran & Carol West
Nils & Marjorie Westerberg
Arvid & Nancy Westfall
David & Mardelle Westley
Paul & Lavonne Westlund
Walter & Bessie Westoby
Peter & Susan Westrum
John & Sharon Wey
Wallace & Gaylyn Whalin
James & Dorothy Wheatley
Nancy Wheeler
Al & Margaret Wheeler
Carol Whisler
David & Janice Whisler
Steve & Kathryn Whitacre
Clyde & Lois Whitby
Dorothy White

Hope White
Pamela White
Philip & Carol White
Steven White
Robert & Rebecca Whitesides
Richard & Nancy Whitmire
Gordon & Marilee Whitney
Henry & Virginia Whitney
Claudia Whittle
Katherine Wieck
Marinus & Elizabeth Wiering
Kenneth & Patricia Wiggers
Joy Wilcox
James & Mary Wilderman
Patricia Wilkendorf
Bruce & Linda Wilkinson
Robert & Lois Wilkinson
Thomas & Elizabeth Willett
Ann Williams
Kathryn Williams
Albert & Eunice Williams
Ben & Elma Williams
Donald & Terry Williams
Gordon Williams
John Williams
Kenneth & Barbara Williams
Larry & Cindy Williams
Paul & Linda Williams
Mark Willis
John & Susan Wilner
Clyde Wilson
Darryl & Lael Wilson
James & Joyce Wilson
John Wimbish
Dorcas Winfrey
Diane Winkfield
Leon & Lola Winter
Mary Wise
David & Robin Witmer
Joel & Heidi Witt
Bruce & Betty Witteveen
Cornelius & Doris Wolfe
Elmer & Beverly Wolfenden
Marguerite Wollerton
Vida Wolter
Cary Wong
Cheryl Wood
Linda Woodden
Marvin & Gladys Woods
George & Phyllis Woodward
Duke & Marian Wooldridge
David & Gayle Worley
Naomi Wray
Robert & Dorothy Wright
Betsy Wrisley
Ronald Wroblewski
Diane Wroge
James & Ellen Wroughton
James & Gloria Wroughton
William & Deborah Wulff
Mildred Wylie
Paul & Margaret Wyse
Ronald & Lucille Yaddaw
John & Ruth Yarbrough
R Wayne & Valerie Yates
Susan Yeasting
Gordon & Lorelee Yoell
James & Kathleen Yost
Larry & Willa Yost
E Virginia Young
Billy & E Irene Young
Bruce & Carolyn Young
Philip & Sandra Young
Scott & Lois Youngman
Forrest & Margaret Zander
Larry & Jeanne Zaugg
Lorin & Marguerite Zechiel
Kenneth & Ella Zell
Ernest & Gladys Zellmer
Donald & Irmgard Ziemer
Marilou Zimmerman
Virginia Zion
Kenneth & Ada Zook
Carol Zylstra